WATCH YOUR HEAD

WATCH YOUR HEAD

WRITERS & ARTISTS RESPOND TO THE CLIMATE CRISIS

EDITED BY
KATHRYN MOCKLER
WITH

MADHUR ANAND, STEPHEN COLLIS, JENNIFER DORNER, CATHERINE
GRAHAM, ELENA JOHNSON, CANISIA LUBRIN, KIM MANNIX, JUNE PAK,
SINA QUEYRAS, SHAZIA HAFIZ RAMJI, RASIQRA REVULVA, YUSUF SAADI,
SANCHARI SUR, & JACQUELINE VALENCIA

COACH HOUSE BOOKS, TORONTO

first edition

Canada Council   Conseil des Arts
for the Arts   du Canada

ONTARIO ARTS COUNCIL
CONSEIL DES ARTS DE L'ONTARIO
an Ontario government agency
un organisme du gouvernement de l'Ontario

Canadä

Published with the generous assistance of the Canada Council for the Arts and the Ontario Arts Council. Coach House Books also acknowledges the support of the Government of Canada through the Canada Book Fund.

Every effort has been made to request permission from rightsholders to reissue the selections in Watch Your Head. *If you hold the rights to any of these pieces and haven't granted permission, please email editor@chbooks.com and we'll rectify this in future reprints.*

LIBRARY AND ARCHIVES CANADA CATALOGUING IN PUBLICATION

Title: Watch your head : writers & artists respond to the climate crisis / edited by Kathryn Mockler ; with Madhur Anand, Stephen Collis, Jennifer Dorner, Catherine Graham, Elena Johnson, Canisia Lubrin, Kim Mannix, June Pak, Sina Queyras, Shazia Hafiz Ramji, Rasiqra Revulva, Yusuf Saadi, Sanchari Sur, Jacqueline Valencia.
Other titles: Watch your head (Toronto, Ont.)
Names: Mockler, Kathryn, editor.
Identifiers: Canadiana (print) 2020032389X | Canadiana (ebook) 20200324012 | ISBN 9781552454121 (softcover) | ISBN 9781770566590 (EPUB) | ISBN 9781770566446 (PDF)
Subjects: LCSH: Climatic changes—Literary collections. | LCSH: Global warming—Literary collections. | LCSH: Environmental protection in art. | LCSH: Art, Modern—21st century.
Classification: LCC PS8237.C65 W38 2020 | DDC 808.8/036—dc23

Watch Your Head is available as an ebook: ISBN 978 1 77056 659 0 (EPUB); ISBN 978 1 77056 644 6 (PDF)

Proceeds from the sales of *Watch Your Head* will be donated to RAVEN and Climate Justice Toronto.

TABLE OF CONTENTS

INTRODUCTION

Everyone has the responsibility to respond to this crisis.

– Rita Wong

BACKGROUND

The seed of this project was planted at a protest. On September 7, 2019, Kathryn Mockler organized a reading with eight writers for an environmental group hosting a protest at Simcoe Park during the Toronto International Film Festival. The day-long event included music, readings, and art performances. As the sky threatened rain and most people in the area were enjoying the festival, the event itself was small – about fifteen or so were in attendance along with a few passersby.

But that didn't matter. Once each performer took the mic, the size of the audience and the greyness of the autumn day fell away. It was just the writers, their words, and their messages, which were captured on video. The readers included Margaret Christakos, Adam Giles, Catherine Graham, Hege Jakobsen Lepri, Khashayar Mohammadi, Terese Mason Pierre, Rasiqra Revulva, and Todd Westcott.

An online platform was needed to share this moving and powerful event, and so *Watch Your Head* was born at watchyourhead.ca. The title comes from the language of caution signs that warn those in the vicinity of known and preventable dangers in the hopes of avoiding a catastrophic event that could lead to injury or death. This seemed like a fitting title for a project about the climate emergency.

Once the site went live, several writers and artists offered to lend their support to the project, forming an editorial collective that would publish creative works focused on climate justice and the climate crisis. Alana Wilcox from Coach House Books approached us about publishing a print anthology and several editors from the *Watch Your Head* collective joined the print anthology editorial team: Madhur Anand, Stephen Collis, Jennifer Dorner, Catherine Graham, Elena

Johnson, Canisia Lubrin, Kim Mannix, Kathryn Mockler, June Pak, Sina Queyras, Shazia Hafiz Ramji, Rasiqra Revulva, Yusuf Saadi, Sanchari Sur, and Jacqueline Valencia.

At the heart of the *Watch Your Head* project in all of its manifestations – website, print anthology, readings, events – is a desire not only to draw attention to the present and future implications of the climate crisis, but also to inspire people to get involved in climate justice action and solidarity initiatives.

CLIMATE JUSTICE

Climate justice acknowledges the fact that the radical ecological and biospheric transformation currently unfolding on our planet is predicated upon social inequalities, and embeds future inequalities. In other words, the extractive industrial practices driving global warming and all its associated depletions are an extension of a historical colonization built upon the theft of the lands and bodies of Indigenous and Black peoples, which continues today by displacing largely Indigenous peoples from their lands and will, as the climate warms, disproportionately impact racialized communities, so-called developing nations in the Global South, and other marginalized people. A climate-justice approach insists that questions of colonization and decolonization, racism, anti-Blackness, and other forms of forcibly maintained social inequalities, exclusions, and persecutions cannot be separated from the question of the climate and the planet's eroding natural environment. It is not insignificant that we write these words in the midst of a global pandemic, which has most severely impacted racialized communities, low-income communities, migrant workers, long-term-care residents, and other vulnerable people. It is not insignificant that at this moment some of the largest and most intense anti-Black-racism protests in decades, and concomitant police violence, are happening. Climate justice, and much of the work in this anthology, acknowledges these complexities, contradictions, and convergence points.

In part, this leads to a questioning of the Anthropocene – a term you will not frequently encounter in this anthology – as a lens for understanding the present. The Anthropocene proposes a universal: human activity did this; we all did this. As Kathryn Yusoff writes in *A Billion Black Anthropocenes or None*, 'To be included in the "we" of the Anthropocene is to be silenced by a claim to universalism that fails to notice its subjugations.'[1] *Watch Your Head* strives to avoid such silencing universalism, offering instead a diverse and wide-ranging response to the experience of the current crisis.

Poet Rita Wong's public statement upon her sentencing (to four weeks in jail) for defying a court injunction and blockading the entrance to the Trans Mountain Pipeline's Westridge Marine Terminal can serve as a paradigm for climate justice, directing us to new frames of allyship within our fraught condition. It is also a powerful inspiration to hear a writer speak so directly of the necessity of action: 'I did this because we're in a climate emergency.'[2] Her declaration of responsibilities – to ancestors, to the salmon, to the trees, the ocean, and to the life-giving waters all around us – is the basis of her redefinition of justice. Justice, Wong argues, from the unceded territories upon which she stands and lives, must at the very least acknowledge the equal validity of the rule of natural law and Coast Salish Indigenous law, alongside the sentencing court's colonial rule of law. Wong's climate justice is thus predicated upon a 'reciprocal relationship with the land and water,' and 'is a rule of law that works primarily from a place of love and respect, not from fear of authority and punishment':

> Our ceremony that morning was an act of spiritual commit-
> ment, of prayer, of artistic expression, of freedom of expression,
> an act of desperation in the face of climate crisis, an act of

1. Kathryn Yusoff. *A Billion Black Anthropocenes or None*. University of Minnesota Press. 2018.

2. Rita Wong. 'Rita Wong's Public Sentencing Statement.' Talonbooks. 18 August 2019. https://talonbooks.com/news/rita-wong-s-public-sentencing-statement.

allegiance with the earth's natural laws, and a heartfelt attempt to prevent mass extinction of the human race.[3]

SCIENCE, SOCIETY, AND LANGUAGE

The scientific basis of climate change dates back to 1896, when Svante Arrhenius proposed a connection between fossil-fuel combustion and increases in global temperature. Perhaps better known are Charles David Keeling's observations taken at Mauna Loa Observatory in the late 1950s, which gave rise to the Keeling Curve.[4] The impacts of climate change on the earth and its inhabitants are also very well known. Numerous reports have been issued by the Intergovernmental Panel on Climate Change, the most recent of which calls for 'rapid, unprecedented, and far-reaching' changes to all aspects of society.[5]

Our predictions of climate change come from global circulation models, which conceptualize the complex numerical biogeophysical underpinnings of climate, but these modes of prediction can only go so far in terms of effecting societal change. It is important to refine these models, particularly in examining how global changes can have local impacts that are easier for humanity to act upon, but, even then, human behaviour unfolds at different levels and in different dimensions from the computational logic of such models. The science of climate change has been communicated to governments and society time and time again, through all sorts of media, but the messages are not being acted upon. Predicting dire future consequences is not working, which places science at a strange standstill. This is not because science is uncertain or inadequate, but change is impeded by the power and privilege of the sectors of

3. Ibid.

4. Charles D. Keeling (1960). 'The concentration and isotopic abundances of carbon dioxide in the atmosphere.' *Tellus*, 12 (2): 200–203. doi:10.3402/tellusa.v12i2.9366.

5. The Intergovernmental Panel on Climate Change. 'Global Warming of 1.5°C.' United Nations. https://www.ipcc.ch/sr15/. Accessed 11 June 2020.

society that addressing climage change would disrupt.

Interventions into the making of climate data could be one way to bridge the gap, as Adam Dickinson does in his poem 'Perspiration, a Conspiracy,' which interrogates the physiological climate change impacts on the human body (rising temperature) using the language of poetry.

The recent move of the *Guardian* to change their style guide ('climate change' is now 'climate crisis' or 'global heating') highlights the importance of language to create the necessary cultural shift.[6] Writers and artists are needed not to correct our language of what is known, but to use it, like the complex and messy data it is, to create new forms and ideas, and to explore those spaces of unknowing, the much-needed imagining of climate futures. Ultimately, for the insights brought to humanity by artists on the issue of climate change to be fully realized, conversations between artists and scientists must continue.

WATCH YOUR HEAD

The poems, stories, essays, and artwork collected in this anthology by necessity offer a broad range of responses to the current crisis: writers and artists give voice to widely shared fears and the enveloping sense of the uncanniness of our times; they attempt to imagine the unimaginable; they remind us what we can and must attend to, and what we are unavoidably attached to; they explore the limits and possibilities of language in the face of catastrophe, loss, and grief; and, of course, they name names and take numbers, looking for payback.

The increasing sense of the precariousness of life, the care and attention this calls for, and the admission of complicities we must face are a common topic – what Allison Cobb calls, with a deft line

---

6. Damian Carrington. 'Why the *Guardian* is changing the language it uses about the environment.' 17 May 2019. https://www.theguardian.com/environment/2019/may/17/why-the-guardian-is-changing-the-language-it-uses-about-the-environment

break, 'that sense of hanging / on,' despite 'the blood's toxic cargo.' Anna Swanson's take on the ledge-factor of the climate emergency, in her poem 'I Am Writing a Spell for Your Nervous System,' is to invoke the careful listening of 'baby monitors / tuned to the evening news.' But that listening is revelatory, giving us access to 'geologic time … breathing hard.' Temporal measurements, as the poets attempt to assess the *nowness* of their now, are everywhere, from Jessica Le's desperate mantra 'it's not too late. it's not too late. it's not too late' to Manahil Bandukwala's musing on the 'precious hours / at the end / of the world' and Kunjana Parashar's awareness of the proximity of life, identity, and the unfolding disaster: 'I was born … somewhere around the confirmed end of Javan tigers.'

The inevitable complicities – and troubling and embodied proximities to the disaster – concern many of our contributors. Ellen Chang-Richardson's speaker in 'Meltwater Basin' feels 'wrapped, in polyurethane,' and Jessica Magonet, in 'Revolution,' considers the 'crude oil / on my hands' as they contemplate their upcoming flight.

The very everydayness of these effects does not dispel their impact; in fact, it heightens it, and the poets, fiction and essay writers, and artists in this anthology excel at giving voice to the complexities that have become an ordinary part of our lives – from Nikki Reimer's speaker declaring in 'I Still Want Eyelid Bees' that they are '"sad" about "mass species death," but will "still use plastic strips" / to "wax my back mole,"' to the characters in Sarah Mangle's comic 'Weird' who contemplate climate change during a conversation about the weather, to the speaker of Carleigh Baker's story 'Grey Water' writing to a distant and perhaps wayward lover: 'you have boulevards, I have baths. We are terrible.' The context here of course is the problem of dwindling waters in a warming world, and their radically uneven distribution. Baker's narrator says:

> You know, I've seen photos of the drought situation in California. Comparison between now and ten years ago: reservoirs, riverbeds, lakes. Have you seen the photos? The situation looks

pretty grim. But last time we visited, I remember people watering their lawns, boulevards with lush green grass, the long, long shower we took together the morning before we left. All the swimming pools we passed over on our flight home, little blue tiles crammed into an uncomfortable crush of stucco and asphalt. Water is everything, and they don't have much.

When it comes to imagining the unimaginable – something we often expect to be the purview of writers and artists contemplating ecological crises – we find here instead the problem, as articulated by Anna Swanson, that 'some futures are no longer / unimaginable.' The postmodern adage – that it is easier to imagine the end of the world (Hollywood has flooded us with these images) than the end of capitalism – comes into play here: we know the drill when it comes to the apocalypse. We get glimpses of it in Jana Prikryl's poem 'Snapshot,' where 'the needle at the top of the Chrysler Building / is visible now and then under whitecaps' and a 'coral garden Central Park' lies 'dreaming at the bottom.' And in Aude Moreau's photographic project *La ligne bleue* (*The blue line*), which 'proposes to draw a line of blue light across the night skyline of Lower Manhattan' measured at sixty-five metres from the ground to 'correspond to the projected sea level if all of the ice on the planet were to melt.'

But more often than not we find grief here in the face of the no-longer-unimaginable: Barry Pottle documenting melting ice in *De-Iced*, a photo series that attempts to bring awareness 'to and of climate change and global warming from an urban Inuk artist's perspective' or Jacob Wren contemplating the difficulty of writing when the idea that 'someone might continue to read [their work] far into the future' becomes less and less plausible.

The work collected here also suggests that conscious attention is as important as the imagining of possibilities – but it may also be the

---

7. Barry Pottle. '*De-Iced* Artist Statement.' *Watch Your Head.* https://www.watchyourhead.ca/watch-your-head/photography-barry-pottle. 10 January 2020.

case that the imagination is one of the key resources attention draws upon. Carrianne Leung, in a moving personal essay, 'Writing in a Dangerous Time,' draws these threads together beautifully:

> We know that a writer needs to attend to the world, and I do. But I do so lately with an intensity that can only be described as a last gasp, as if all this will fall away like illusion at any moment, and I must remember it to record properly … And isn't that the whole point of literature? To show us to ourselves and keep pursuing this question: what does it mean to be human?

Leung goes on to suggest that 'to be human' is to take up the work of 'fostering good relations … Writing possible futures must necessarily lead us back to the concept of relationship, and this includes non-human life forms.' The relational may be the dominant thread in this anthology – the attention to connection that the intensity of the moment (when things begin to fall apart and drift away) demands.

We see it in Kevin Adonis Browne's photo series *The Coast*, which portrays what he calls 'the aesthetics of environmental erasure – of what goes, what remains, and what is brought back to us on the tide.'

And it's what Kazim Ali finds out at the Jenpeg Generating Station and dam, at Cross Lake in northern Manitoba, where Pimicikamak Elder Jackson Osborne tells Ali how culture, language, and water interconnect across the land: disrupt one and the others are disrupted too.

Then there are the birds heard by Jónína Kirton in her poem 'for the birds,' who sing out the benediction '*all my relations*,' in 'a poem about the web of connections.' The poem draws upon its special capacities of address here too, of listening and responding to the more-than-human, as in Gary Barwin's series of 'goodbyes'; in Ching-In Chen's 'Lantern Letter,' with its desire to 'vow an impossible hello'; and in Erin Robinsong's 'Anemone,' in which the speaker attempts 'to think / with anemones' – and 'without money.' Finally, CAConrad, listening to recordings of now extinct animals in 'For the Feral Splendour That Remains,' invites us to 'fall in love with the world,' at the very moment we appear to be lending a hand in its destruction:

in a future life
would we like to
fall in love with the
world as it is with
no recollection
of the beauty
we destroy
today

The literary work, as it always does, approaches its 'contents' (even when they involve a dire climate emergency) through the play of its linguistic 'forms,' exemplified by Margaret Christakos's anaphoristic repetitions of the conditional word 'whether' to summon that ultimate condition, the 'weather,' in her poem 'Whether the Heavens Break.' When the poet considers the language they bring to such an emergency, the questions proliferate. Rae Armantrout, in 'Speculative Fiction,' offers up this quandary:

In the future we will face new problems.

How will we represent the variety of human types
once all the large animals are gone?

As sly as a mother
as hungry as an orphan?

Jordan Abel, in 'Empty Spaces (3),' a work written at the intersection of fiction and poetry, offers another method: to re-occupy the spaces emptied by colonization (in this case, via the textual body of James Fenimore Cooper's *The Last of the Mohicans*) to create new and ultimately more meaningful emptinesses – by reversing the engineering of colonization, and occupying the texts through which colonial displacements and evacuations were originally enacted.

None of the writers or artists here shy away from confrontation or the forces that have led us to the present brink. The situation can be and is named bluntly: 'it comes down to money' (Elee Kraljii Gardiner and Andrew McEwan write in 'Debating Foundations'). Eshrat Erfanian points to the pervasiveness of capitalism's reach in her series *Tres-pass*, where the addresses of Middle Eastern oil refineries are juxtaposed with landscape photos taken at sites in Ontario and Quebec, polluted by mining companies in the 1950s and now being developed into luxury retirement communities. In her photographic series *Sleeping*, Shelley Niro's 'Sleeping Warrior Dreams of Pastures and Power' while Mercedes Eng side-eyes 'the apocalypse that yt people keep making movies about,' which is not, and never has been, the apocalypse so many have had to endure for at least 500 long colonial years. Jody Chan returns us to the scene of protest, advising us 'to attend your five-hundredth rally,' if that's what it takes, and 'to allow yourself *I don't know how to fix it*,' but nevertheless, 'to allow an entire future this way, day by unimaginable day, to arrive.' Also deeply stirring is the barely suppressed rage and righteous anger of fifteen-year-old activist Ira Reinhart-Smith, part of a youth lawsuit against the federal government of Canada for its failure to act on climate change, who will not abide the 'ashen fields' produced by business as usual.

The poems, stories, essays, and artwork collected in *Watch Your Head* are warnings to be heeded, directions given, field notes from the midst of the disaster, offers of refuge, shelter in the storm, high ground marked out, refugia demarcated and carefully tended, pleas, modes, and methods of survival – when survival seems ever so much in doubt. *Field notes* is perhaps in the end the correct term for this work, in the sense in which Simone Dalton deploys the concept in 'Notes from a Small Place.' In Dalton's case, observing the 'migratory pull' – or perhaps push – shared by human beings and birds such as egrets, these are field notes on climate migration, displacement, and the extractive-colonial aftermath in 'a world wrung by loss.' So it is with much of the work gathered in this anthology.

Ours is a 'crisis of consciousness,' Dalton continues: 'We cannot care about what we do not believe; we cannot act if we are not aware.' But the work in *Watch Your Head* also moves out beyond the matrices of consciousness-raising to inhabit the turbulent spaces, in Jónína Kirton's words, 'between observation and intervention,' where we find our way to appropriate actions, or we don't, and suffer the consequences. What is in evidence here is that as long as the writer can write, the artist can make art, the speaker can speak, and the singer can sing, the warning will be given. Watch. Your. Head.

Stephen Collis
Madhur Anand
Kathryn Mockler

WE WILL TELL THEM OF OUR DOMINION
Terese Mason Pierre

First, we will tell them of our dominion.
We will tell them of the web peeling back
in the heavens, the sun's maw radiating
We will tell them we can see the air
We will tell them green turned brown and grey
We will tell them green covered the earth
We will tell them of plastic islands
We will tell them of sands too hot to inhabit,
We will tell them of where people
cannot hold their breath forever

We will tell them of undulating obituaries
We will tell them of backroom deals, of slow-moving cogs
We will tell them of childhood depression
We will tell them of corporate footprints,
handprints, fingers in pies, stained red
We will tell them of mass delusion
We will tell them of moral misbehaviour
We will tell them of fears for marble over feather and fur

We will tell them about the non-identity problem
We will tell them of the powerful two-faced
We will tell them why the scientists cried
We will tell them why the philosophers cried
We will tell them why the parents cried

We will tell them of carbon-dioxide
shouts, of splintered protests
We will tell them of tear gas, of turned heads
We will tell them of laws broken

We will tell them of backs broken
We will tell them of turning, turning

Later, we will tell them the oil barons are dead
We will tell them guardians fought back
We will tell them a panacea was birthed from the Amazon ash
We will tell them blood is not translucent, but still pumping
We will tell them the ocean is still loud
We will tell them we relocated the sacred
We will tell them we refined our brains
We will tell them the sun is everything
We will tell them we were sorry
We will tell them we know why the sky is blue.

EMPTY SPACES (3)
Jordan Abel

On the shore, there is a deep, narrow chasm that leads down into some other, darker place. On the shore, there are black rocks and roots and mud and tree stumps and broken bones and broken branches. On the shore, a river cuts through the trees. Sometimes there is a moment. Sometimes there are other, softer places. At this very moment, there is lightning and then there is a tumbling in the air a mile above us. At this very moment, white lightning breaks open the sky and runs straight through the open heavens into some other place. In the forest, there is a deep hollow. A gully with a dozen branching pathways to follow. There are no shapes here other than the trees. There is nothing here that breaks apart. Somewhere, deep in the gully, there is a soft, dark place. Sometimes, a hundred feet up in the air, there is just light and clouds and cold droplets of water. Sometimes right angles run parallel to the river. Sometimes right angles cut through the forest. Sometimes the water cuts through the rocks near the northern summit. Sometimes the water works through these rocks. Some hundred feet in the air there is no danger; there is only the broken and the splintered and the open, sprawling land. There is scattered driftwood and the scent of roses and mossy rocks and tree stumps and broken branches and wet leaves. There are glimpses of roses and rocks and shrubs. There is a steep, rugged ascent. Somewhere, there is a path that winds among the black rocks and trees. Somewhere out there is the scent of roses. Somewhere out there is another forest, another river, another mouth. Somewhere out there is the taste of danger. Somewhere out there is the open, sprawling land and the endless horizon. Somewhere out there is the wilderness. Somewhere out there, at some reasonable distance, are scenes of greenery and nature and glimpses of mountain ranges that disappear just as suddenly as they appear. Among the mossy rocks and the broken tree branches, there are mounds of black earth and other rocks and other driftwood. Somewhere, there is an islet and another islet and a clear sheet of water and bald rocks just beneath the surface. There are forests and straits and islets and rocks and somewhere in the air is the scent of roses. In the forest, there are deep, soft places. In the forest, there are hollows and ravines and winding rivers. The rivers connect themselves to other rivers, other lakes, other inlets and streams and waterfalls. In between the rivers, there are sometimes mounds of earth. There are sometimes great expanses of trees and shrubs and brush. In the forest, there are fractured rivers. Rivers that break apart again and again until there is barely a stream running through the thick parts of the forest. In the deeper parts of the river, though, there is more tumbling. At this very moment, the river pours into a wide fissure where it just becomes more water between rocks. In this river – the river that splits open over and over again – there are sunken bodies and bald rocks. Above this river, there is a deep, roaring cavern and there is the scent of roses in the air. There is light and straight, naked rocks and immovable trees and the taste of danger. In this forest, the river will split again and again. In this forest, the river is ragged with rocks and broken branches and driftwood. In this forest, the river cuts silently through the ravine. In this forest, the scent from the water intersects with the scent of roses floating above somewhere up in the air. This forest is full. The upper air, where it drifts over the tops of the ragged trees, is full of sounds. Just where it breaks over the tops of trees there are slow, intermingling drifts of sounds and scents that brush over the clearing some seventy or eighty feet up in the air. Mossy rocks and logs and rivers that cut through the forest. Mounds of earth and narrow fissures. Bottom land and little ponds and inlets and a brook that shoots through the trees, spreading through the afternoon. There is a bellowing somewhere in the forest above the river. There are moments where the light stretches out across the horizon and fills up the sky. A light that turns the clouds pink and orange and yellow. There is light spreading over the soft expanse of the forest. There are precipices and adjacent lakes and headwaters and summits. There is a fierceness here in the forest. There is a fierceness that drifts along in the rivers. These rivers are full to the brim. These waters stream down to our feet. In six hours the water from this river will reach the lake at the base of the mountain. In six hours a few bodies will wash up on the shore of that lake. Bodies swell in this water. The water in the woods and on the great lakes and in the higher parts of the sea. The stream stretches out horizontally until the current flows upward like blood at the throat. In these waters, the bodies clump together and the stench carries up into the air. In the short distance in between the lake and forest is a shore. There is a shore at the base of the mountain where swollen, broken bodies clump together. There are black rocks and deep shadows and rustling leaves in the forest. There is a mist drifting through the trees. There are shores. There is a soft mist floating just above the surface. The breath of the stream. The sharp reflections. The woods and the bodies and the taste of danger. These shores are full of throats that have been cut, limbs that have been severed. These woods are full of bodies and bones and moss and trees and broken branches and rustling leaves and soft, silvery wind. Gliding above somewhere up in the impenetrable darkness is the scent of roses. Somewhere there is the sound of rushing waters. Somewhere in the night there is a deep stillness. At some point, the moonlight touches the water and riverbed and the broken bodies. At this moment, the light hangs in the air just above the bodies. These woods are full. There are bright, moonlit bodies; there is light from some other, colder place. At another moment, there would be sweetness on this shore. At another moment, there would be an unmingled sweetness of air that sinks into the bright, moonlit waters. At this moment, there is a stillness. At this very moment, the moonlight touches the bodies on the shore and there is a deep stillness. There is a soft, silvery wind that drifts through the forest onto the shore. There are tall trees. There is mud and broken branches and mossy rocks and tree stumps and driftwood and a broken pile of bodies. There is a stillness here on the shore. There is lightning and then there is stillness. There are echoes that rush through the forest until they disappear. A mile above there is a tumbling. A mile above seems like some other, softer place. In the water of the lake, there is the bright reflection of moonlight. A cold light from somewhere other than here. Some light touches the dead. Some light carries us to some other, softer place. Some light fills us with hope and warmth. Some light lasts forever. Somewhere up in the darkness there is the scent of roses. Somewhere in the darkness there is a soft, silvery wind. Some flames flicker out. Some waters carry bodies. Some waters are still. Somewhere in the velocity of the uproar there is a current of air. There is an unmingled sweetness that sinks in to the forest. The shore is full of bodies. The blood as natural as mud. The gully and the soft, dark places of the forest and the glassy waters and the sunken bodies and the shore and the moonlight and the pink clouds and the muddy roots and the severed limbs and the soft, silvery wind and the taste of danger and the black rocks between the mounds of earth and the glittering stars and the open air floating over the forest and the valley and the stream overflowing onto the banks and the tumbling water and the branching pathways and the wet leaves and nearly everything in between. Here, the rushing water washes bones and the waters of the river run in to the mountain lake. When the sun is directly above us, a shadow from the canopy will spread over the lake, creating a dark current with a deep hue. When the sun is directly above us, these waters become healing waters. Tomorrow, the sun will be directly above us and we will be healed by these waters. When the sun is directly above us, these currents will branch silently into the dark parts of the lake. When the sun is directly above us. When light touches all of the soft, dark places. When light spreads like a wave through the forest. When the forest starts to break open. When trees collapse. When branches break. When bodies are covered over by the earth. When there is a deep, cool wind. When there is a current of air, there will also be silent motion. The forest is pulled by the soft, silvery wind. The broken branches are swept up in that current. There is the sound from the rushing water drifting through the air. From somewhere deep in the forest, there are voices again. From somewhere deep in the forest, there are more soft bodies, more sharp objects, more breath in the air. As the air flows up from the deep, soft places of the forest, the sound of rushing water can be heard again. Distant sounds that come from the branching river. The broken river with the clear, upstream water runs through the forest beneath some low bushes. Branches wave in the current of this river. Some call this river by a name. For many moments, the branches bend in the eddies, and the arm of the river turns toward itself. For many moments, the name of the river hangs in the air. Every few yards, bubbles appear on the surface, are filled with light, and disappear. At the shore, there is a dead silence, and then there are low voices. Somewhere under the ragged treetops is the growing sound of voices but the voices are obscured. Somewhere on the river, bark can be seen floating along with the current. The down stream current. The far down current, sinking again beneath the air. There is a current that swells and sinks and crashes against the rocks, echoing through the vaults of forest and the sweetness of nature. Above the canopy, bodies can be seen drifting through the trees. There is quiet motion; there is breath. In the caverns below, there is air that rises up to meet those bodies. The bodies are just flesh drifting through the air, crushing the broken branches that have already fallen to the forest floor. The air. The sparks. The flames. The smoke. The cool evening breeze sweeps around the bodies. Any breath. Any fire. Any thunder rumbling beyond the distant hills. Any surface. Any signal. Any water. Any alarm far down the current of the river. Which bodies can be trusted? Which breath sounds the sweetest? Which connections can be formed from these soft groupings of flesh? Which company will find their way out of this forest? Which pathways will stretch on without ending? Which pathways will be hazardous? The air sinks into the caverns below and the voices sink too. Which current glides toward fortune and which current turns treacherous? The river plunges into the ravine and the mist rises like smoke. For a few moments, the mist is the smoke before it falls back into the river. For a few moments, there is a plume of water crested by the light that cuts through the forest. Somewhere in the trees, there are leaves falling onto a path. A path that winds through the trees and around the river. Behind the curvature of the path is a dark, wooded outline and a soft, silvery wind. The open heavens and the drifting vapours and the broken treetops and the sullen sounds and the evening atmosphere and the blazing fire and the deep laughter and the broken rocks and the roaring cavern and the rushing water and the impenetrable darkness and the water glimmering in the moonlight and the hills and the gloom and the moving surfaces and the quiet uneasiness and the wooded outlines and the silvery wind and the broken branches and soft, dark places in the forest. In this gully, there is a darkness that can only be tasted. Another tree. Another body. Another knot. Another notch. But which tree? Which body? Which knot? Which notch? Which soft expanse of trees? Which position of the sun? Which direction of the water? Which hesitation before speech? Which flesh enters into the river? Some say that all the knots of pine can be counted. Some say there will always be another mouth. When the spirits rustle the leaves of other forests. When the dead listen. When there are no more noises. When the blood is hot. When black smoke drifts through the camp like a fog. When the vapours are inhaled. When the clouds settle onto the trees. When white lightning breaks open the sky above us. When the forest bursts into flames. Somewhere in the gully, there are naked voices and a wall of heat. Breath and silence and breath again. In the deepest hollow of the gully there is fire. At the edge of the lake there is a narrow, deep cavern in the rock. Some day bodies will spread over either side of the great lakes. In the west, there will be as many bodies as there are leaves on the trees. In the fields, bodies bloom like fire. On the broad side of the trail, the air tastes like copper and the holy lake is full of bodies. Bodies and air and flesh and moonlight and breath and fire in the fields. Numberless bodies and songs and voices. Tonight, the stars will shine. Tonight, the evergreens will grow. Bodies will spread out across the soft expanse of forest and beyond the western horizon as seen through the branches of trees and the west will arrive. Above the pines, the sky is bright and pink and delicate. Where are the deep shadows?

What forms out of the damp morning air? What bitterness? What glory? What country? The rippling stream bends toward every vista. The sun sets in a flood. Here, coolness spreads through the beach. The bodies and the broken masses of rock and the distant western hills and the spectacle of darkness and the pure exhalations of spring and the eastern shore and the north island and the mountains and silent moments and the shaggy outlines of the tall pines and nearly everything in between. From the woods. From the darkness. From the broken masses of rock. From the distant eastern hills. From the north. From the eastern shores that are barely visible in the heat of the afternoon comes a silence that burns like fire. From the southern end. From mountain to mountain. From the eastern bank of the lake. From eye. From body. From witness. From the bodies that see themselves. From the dizzying heights. From the narrow sheets. From truth. From weakness. From speaking. From flame. From the air pouring across the waste waters. From light. From margin. From earth. From broken summits and broken sky. From the broken branches and the mossy rocks and the deep, narrow ravines. From the soft, dark places of the forest. From the blood spilling into the rivers. From the tumbling in the air a mile above us. Below the high and broken summits are countless islands and clear sheets of water running from shore to shore. After all the portage trails winding through the trees. After all the low strands disappearing into the water and reappearing in parallel. After all the hills and the lakes. After all the waterfalls and mists and riverbeds. The morning will approach again tomorrow. The morning approaches again. From this spot, the bodies almost seem to linger in the heat from the afternoon sun. Beyond the miles of unbroken water. Beyond the shores of the lakes. Beyond the danger. Beyond the eastern waters. Beyond the horizon are miles and miles of lakes that intersect and overlap, sharing vessels that glide along the currents. The chasms. The black waters. The shores. Somewhere along the horizon the earth disappears. For a few moments, there is no lake. There are no bodies. There are no mountains. There are no waters. There is no moon. There is no forest. There is only darkness. For just a moment, there is only darkness. For just a moment, all the soft, dark places of the forest disappear into that darkness. Where the light reappears, there are clouds in the sky. There are headlands dotted with countless islands. There are islands surrounded by other islands. There are cliffs and forests and rivers. Sometimes the elevation plunges. Sometimes the waters rise. Sometimes the bodies are no great distance. Sometimes the clouds spill out across the sky. Sometimes there is the scent of roses. Sometimes there is white lightning in the sky a mile in the air above us. Sometimes fires die out. Somewhere deep in the woods there is a dark lake at the bottom of a mountain. There are slow waters here. There are echoes and rocks and fissures and bodies and mounds of earth and shrubs and little ponds and mossy stumps and broken bones and broken bodies. The air is heavy with mist. Branches sway in this air. The air floating and rising and cooling at the base of this mountain. If there is the taste of copper in the air. If there is scattered light from the brush above. If the air floats over the lake. If the west. If the voices. If the bodies. If the soft, silvery wind. If the rocks. If the trees. If the waters here are forever. If the waters here dry up. If the intermingling drifts of air above stretch out to intersect with other winds. The bodies here in the lake are silent and still. Somewhere out there, other bodies are broken. Somewhere waters rush through the woods pulling down trees that stand too close to the shore. Limbs break in those currents, on those rocks. The bodies sink into the lake and resurface somewhere between the rocks and the driftwood and the light. For a moment, the moon is visible. In the heat of the afternoon there is a bellowing from the rushing wind that rises up through the branches and the trees and the shrubs and the broken rocks. Beyond these trees there are just more bodies, just more flesh. Beyond these woods there are countless bodies that spill out into the forest and glide out endlessly into the horizon. Beyond these trees, there are soft voices and light and other bodies and breath. Somewhere in the forest branches break. The air swells. What breaks open out of these sounds? What trust forms from breath? What bitterness hangs in the air? What bodies fill the air with words? What flesh can stand this heat? What footsteps are covered over by the sound from the rushing wind? The rocks and logs and immovable mountains that are almost visible from hundreds of miles away and the driftwood and the trees and the lake and the bodies. If the conversations are overheard, the bodies might break. If the bodies are silent. If there is light shining down on the flesh and the trees and the mossy rocks. If there are echoes of voice that cut through the wind. If the west hangs in the air on this breath, then the water must reflect the light from the moon at midnight. If the west is here at all it is caught up somewhere in the uproar of voices that come from the bodies in the trees. The voices that intersect with each other and cut softly through the silence. If the west is to be made, then the bodies will make it. For a few moments, the stars will light up a pathway that winds through the forest and past the lake and between the mountains. For a few moments, all bodies become lost in the smoke. Flames can be seen through the branches. Through the numberless branches and the broken tree limbs and the black rocks and the mounds of earth and the salt lake. Sometimes when the sun sets, the waters from the lake will look like wildfire. But the sun is not setting and waters here only reflect the flames in the forest. Somewhere out there, away from the shore, there is a clear sheet of water and bald rocks just beneath the surface. Somewhere out there, above the water, there is a tumbling in the air a mile above us. Sometimes these waters are full to the brim. Sometimes salt grows in these waters. The water in the lakes and the rivers and the streams and the waterfalls. Sometimes after all this fire there is the taste of copper in the air. Sometimes there is the taste of danger. On the shore, there are only bodies. On the shore there is breath and there is fire and there is burning flesh and there are voices. At the furthest edges of the lake there is another shore. Another quiet shore where there are as many bodies as there are trees. Here, there is light and stillness and glimpses of grey smoke billowing over the tops of trees in the distance. In the far distance, there is another clear sheet of water, another shore, another islet, another mouth. In the far distance, all the clouds of smoke seem to drift into each other, seem to drift through each other. Voices can be heard somewhere out in the forest. For all the fragments of driftwood along the shore. For all the dark mounds of earth and wet rocks and broken branches and intersecting lines of sight. For all the right angles that cut across each other until there is a moment where they intersect. For all the leaves falling to the ground. For all the broken rocks and immovable trees and deep, narrow ravines and soft, dark places. For every cloud that breaks apart. For every leaf that falls from a tree. For every broken body. For every mound of flesh. For every limb. For every drop of blood. For every cheek pressed against the mossy trunk of a tree. Beneath the broken clouds is a steep, rugged descent and a trail of bodies spilling down into the forest and into the lake. There are no sounds anymore except for the crackling of the fire in the woods. There are no shores other than these shores. There are no bodies other than these bodies. There is no flesh other than this flesh. In earlier seasons, flowers would bloom on this shore by the woods overlooking the deep stillness of the lake. Today, the blood blooms in this water. Blood and salt and expanding sheets of dark water. Blood gushed from soft, delicate bodies. Blood floating through the water until it disappears. Blood sinking into the soft, dark places of the forest. Blood and dirt and rocks and branches and rainwater. There are bodies sinking into the lake that look almost like a half-remembered constellation of stars. Here, the soft, silvery winds push the water and bodies through the lake toward the dark, deep places. There is a blackness at the bottom of the lake that seems to absorb any light that might touch it. For a moment the light from the bright, delicate afternoon and the light from the wildfire reach out to this dark place. For a moment, light touches a place it has never touched before. For a moment, the bodies in the lake are lit up again and can be seen very briefly from the shore. For a moment, there is a soft opening for tired epiphany and quiet reflection. For a moment, the flesh is remembered by the water. Beyond the curvature of the shore, there is the dark, wooded outline of the forest. There is rain now in the dark sky and the fires have died out. There are only bright, glowing embers. Glowing orange and red chunks of wood that hiss momentarily in the downpour and slowly turn black and ashen. The smoke from the fire drifts out over the lake and through the forest. Between the trees and the leaves and the broken branches and the mossy rocks. If there is space here in the smoke for voices, then they are softer than before. If there is space for breaking, it is here and now in the rain overlooking the smoke on the dark lake. If there is space between the trees and the black rocks and the shrubs and the driftwood, it is filled with grey smoke and mounds of black earth and the soft, silvery wind. Somewhere above there is a tumbling in the air a mile above us. Somewhere above, there is a soft, silvery wind that disappears into the trees and cuts through the smoke. Some stars can be seen above the lake and through the broken canopy of smouldering trees. Somewhere above, there is light from somewhere other than here. Some colder, darker place. Some bodies. Some branches. Some limbs. Some bark. Some silence. Some dirt. Some blood. Some smoke. Some water. Some distance. Some wilderness. Some danger. Some voices from some other place. From somewhere under the deep stillness of the lake there is a current that rises up to meet the smoke. A current that cuts through the smoke and the cool water and ripples the lake. There is smoke here that drifts just above the surface. There are slow, intermingling drifts of darkness. There is a darkness here that can only be heard. Just above the expanse. Just above the reflections of the glittering stars. Just above the bodies. Just above the water. Just above the smoke. Just above the nakedness out here in the wilderness. Just above the water that has found its way here after winding its way among countless islands and that turned to vapour in the blistering heat of the summer and cut through the side of the mountain. Water that hung in the air before it poured down on the forest. There is a darkness that drifts through the trees. There are bodies that walk through the trees. There is flesh and there is darkness and there are moments when they seem to intertwine and exist only together as one. At this height, the shining stars are just a little closer. At this height, about a quarter-mile from the base of the mountain, the sun burns the tops of trees. If there is a gust of wind that follows the curvature of the valleys and glides up to the black clouds seventy or eighty feet up in the air. If there is the taste of wilderness in the air on the southern shore. If the trees that have fallen in the river sink down to the riverbed. If the thousands of glittering stars above are never quite visible in the light from the afternoon. If the darkness here drifts through the night. If the rocks just below the surface can't quite be seen. If the bodies here are forever. If the lake stretches up like blood at the throat. If the water from the river branches silently into the drifts of darkness. If there are leaves floating in the river. If the blood sprays into the air. If there are voices. If there are parallels between the tree branches. If the waters rise. If a line is drawn. If there are connections between the precipices. If there are no more hills or banks or caverns or ravines. If there is just flesh on the ground and in the mud. If the lake sometimes shines in the light from the sun in the afternoon. If there are roses. If the bodies float down the stream. If there is the taste of danger. If there are moments that intersect with other moments. If the smoke consumes the forest. If the south bank remains a point in space. If the bodies hang in the trees. If a broken line branches into the east. If the light between leaves is just moonlight. If the woods disappear into the night. If there is old light and a bright mist and glassy rocks. If there are caverns in the rocks that lead us into darkness. If there is in fact still a sun after the woods grow dark. If there are ripples in the lake water. If there is fear. If the blood runs like a river. If bark is peeled from a tree. If slow, intermingling drifts of sounds and scents float through the air. If the moon reflects the light from the sun. If there are bodies and land and hunger and fire. If there is a country. If there is a nation. If there is a howling wind in the passageways between the broken rocks. If some other, softer place is not softer at all. If some other, softer place is always just through the trees. If blood is gushed from every body. If the darkness never lifts. If there is a tumbling in the air above us. If the bodies are drained of blood.

If the flesh becomes still. If there are steep pathways between the rocks that lead up the mountain. If there are bodies on those pathways. Bodies in the sun. Bodies reflected on the glassy surfaces of the water. Bodies in the coolness of the night. In the night, the mud will harden and freeze over. The bones in the earth will crust over with frost. Some flesh is as solid as the mountains. Some flesh protrudes from the frozen mud. Some flesh still carries the lingering scent of roses. Some waters freeze over. Some waters become ice. Some frozen voices still cry out in the snowy forest. There will always be voices. There will always be words. There will always be some idea of a country. There will always be a future. There will always be tomorrow. Tomorrow ripples outward across the water. Tomorrow spreads out horizontally along all the soft surfaces. Tomorrow, there will be silence. Tomorrow is a circle. Tomorrow is a line that cuts endlessly through the forest. Tomorrow is a dream that repeats again and again. In the frozen river, there is blood. There are broken bodies and broken bones in the ice. On the shore, there is a flat, black rock below the knee and above the hip bone. There is a skull resting on the frozen stump of a tree trunk. To remove the femur. To extract the gold. To puncture the skin. To see the line that connects the fingers to the ribcage to the jaw bone. The stars will puncture the darkness. The clouds will drift apart. The bones will freeze over. There is a clear sheet of ice and frozen bodies somewhere below the surface. The crisp air and the frozen bones and the silvery clouds and the blood and the icy rocks and the skulls and the cold of winter. Even when the sun is directly above the earth there is still a coolness that spreads through the trees. When the light cuts through the brush. When the forest freezes over. When there is a moment. When the bones seem to disappear from seventy or eighty feet up in the air. When the air is cool and clear. When the bones are swallowed by the snow. When a soft, silvery wind rushes through the branches. When winter finally arrives.

HUMPBACKS, HOWE SOUND
Kathleen McCraken

Beyond these windows the whales are singing.

You touch me in the night,
tell me to listen –
low-frequency clicks and cries,
sonar light.

I know the upward thrust,
humped backs peeling
the surface still

the drive down
where mammal flesh
involves with salt.

Theirs the throb of deep
sea bells, carillon riven
by the harpoon's clipped
load and fire.

Out on the sound
whale clamour, whale lament
diminuendo, ullaloo
sorrow song in blue space.

WHALE-FALL SUSPENSION
Adam Sol

They can create complex localized
ecosystems that supply sustenance
to deep-sea organisms for decades.

The downpour of carcasses slowed and then stopped.
It must be the fault of some sin we committed.
What did we do? And how repent?
Where to find insight and nourishment now
if not from the gifts that have always descended?
Heaven is empty.
The light above, always tempting
for those who are prone to such feelings, now beckoned.
The bravest among us formed expeditions
to explore and, if possible, conquer. But none
returned. Our scientists insist
the atmosphere is toxic. Our sages
swear there are monsters too evil for dreams.
The higher planes are not to be explained.
So we burrow deeper and pray for change.

Epigraph from 'Whale Fall – the strange ecosystem in the ocean,' *Hermanus Online Travel Magazine* (blog), June 12, 2016, https://www.hermanusonline. mobi/hermanus-blog/whale-fall-the-strange-ecosystem-in-the-ocean

HIGH SCHOOL FEVER
Kaie Kellough

brome grass
trespasses into my home in the city
    a flat plain of golden green
rolls through the window. the grass
    curves under the wind. blue widens above.
a single ripped cloud surrenders
    and slinks away. the prairie sprawls forever
until, at its very edge, it drops off a cliff
    and there at the bottom
lie phantom bones translucent in the sun. the prairie repeats
    through these letters, it travels from nowhere
to nowhere, like a poem, from one age to another
    over which, maybe, the cowboy flunkies will –
like a chinook. mournful. really, i don't know
    anything about the prairies i just grew
up there, i don't feel sentimental
    about brome grass, country music, seed catalogues,
midnight meteor showers screened on the big sky, although somehow
    sedans from the 1980s make me weep, sentimentally
a chaperoned slow-dance in the school gym
    that defies sincerity, because
i am no longer fun, or young, or drinking a king can
    in a field off Elbow Drive, or screwing
in a parent's company car, a Lincoln Continental
    Oldsmobile Cutlass Supreme, big Caddy
brown Buick Regal with gold trim, burgundy
    Town Car gleaming sweet and eternal
as rage, as a first electric touch of pussy, as a dying high
    i want to recline
in velour upholstery in a parking lot by the river, flick on
    darkness, extinguish the music, and in the soft nowhere

under the poplar trees, hot box
    until the air is   white waves under the windows,
wafting up the glass, and we are submerged, and we
    lose consciousness as the river carries us
into our fourth decade, the car a junked memory
    that doesn't turn over, sunk to the bottom of the gone never
ever again, goodbye, and i am in my home
    dumb among all i own, in a strange city at midnight,
maple trees out the window, cool rippled
    laughter, cigarette smoke, and French,
whose speakers don't give a shit about John Ware,
    the Black cowboy, or teenage auto-erotic
asphyxiation that ended in unintentional
    suicide, circa 1990,
or me.

cross-legged in front of the chrome
AKAI hi-fi   i sipped hashish smoke. plugged
the coiled cable into the jack –
planted my head in the phones

the cruiser arrived at the station,
police opened the car door and Griffin attempted to flee

their Black mouths opened over my ears
transfixed me with their holy warble in tongues

two police officers picked Mr. Stonechild up
for creating a disturbance. Four days later

the cassette clicked and spun, this communion with slowed
magnetic sound my salvation, sound tongued my auricle

outraged that a young black man
could be fatally shot while complying

in a slow vertiginous whorl, an analogue machine speaking in cyclic
stereo
my cranium was covered in electric needles that reached

the Saskatoon police department
preferred not to know what happened

up through the hole in the ozone layer. the singer's patois
leaped between poles of plutonian midnight winter

a white mob in Lasalle stoned a convoy of Mohawks
mostly women, children

and the unconscious house, the snow burning, the winter moon a

haze of heat
an amplifier's bulb overdriven, melting night

his body was found with just one shoe on;
he had frozen to death on the outskirts

my eyelids low against the glow, green lashes casting shade
over white sub-zero dunes, flakes spiralling down from the stucco

seniors leaving Kahnawake for what they had hoped would be safety,
amid rumours of an impending

ceiling, through a waking dream of being nothing, being a void

ordered to stop or risk being shot. He complied
with the order and turned around. Seconds later

an empty body in which smoke, blue reverberation, and ash float

inside the music was a hiss, the hiss of hash smoke released by heat, the hiss of 3M tape riding a slow reel   the ambient release of doubt in the darkened half of the brain, the dust and static crackling, a hiss that engulfed the sound   a hiss that became a white roar, cloud or air or smoke drubbing inside me, inside of which there must have been a door   inside the cascading foam of Kaieteur analogue memory become white noise   density of whispers in both ears, this   my thesis, there must have been a door inside somewhere   if i could pass through   and find myself in the past   but the whispered babble dropped into a rumble   a pattern, a bassline that skanked froth   and locked with a drum's low kick – maybe the drum's black period was –
but the door was closed, and the music took shape again, mobile architecture lighter than air   brass wafting over the cyclic song, and i listening, feeling almost – ~~found~~
      i'd almost reached through no return to touch   but there was nothing there, only space, an ever-receding gleam, the dying luminosity of Alpha Centauri, winked out of existence like species, but still lingering in the onyx   drip of a dream, maybe. i was dreaming. maybe? the smoke swirled to a drop, the skeletal sound a supple graph of notes, of pure time and form   steady on the air   i am 400 years from home, with stardust and salt mixing in my Rizla. high   by the mute dials' nocturnal   fizzle

GOODBYE
Gary Barwin

Goodbye lungs, surly twins, little trees. Goodbye dark. Goodbye tarmac path. Goodbye each breath, each step. Goodbye buildings, waving people, elevators, and our super, puffing ciggies while mopping floors. Goodbye, he nods, but what about the koalas? We had eucalyptus but now we have fire. Goodbye eucalyptus, goodbye twins with fire and money. Goodbye fire and money, twins and habitat. Goodbye city of Hamilton, Ontario. We walk into the dark, take habitat with us. Goodbye shins against the flames, fingers tangled with sky. Goodbye mouth a river, eyes two islands lost in flood, cars underwater but who can tell? Goodbye speech and sight. Goodbye streets and mortgages, ravines and furrows, furloughs, tongues and mathematics. Goodbye clouds, streetcars filled with fish or birds, our hands gripping oceans. We are leaving now. We are leaving because tangled in this net the ocean comes with us.

TOGETHER WE WILL RISE OR FALL
Jónína Kirton

I wanted to write a poem about cavity dwellers
but it became a poem about trees
and how far from the edge of a shrinking forest is safe

I wanted to write a poem about cavity dwellers
but it became a poem about predators   everyone has to eat

I wanted to write a poem about cavity dwellers
but it became a poem about cohabitation
excavators and non-excavators
predators have memory   some birds have to move

I wanted to write a poem about cavity dwellers
but it became a poem about parental strategies,
the ways in limbs and leaves cavity nesters co-operate

I wanted to write a poem about cavity dwellers
but it became a poem about the way
some humans take too much   forget to say thanks

I wanted to write a poem about cavity dwellers
but it became a poem about nest complexity and conspicuousness,
birds singing in front   behind a scientist counting eggs

I wanted to write a poem about cavity dwellers
but it became a poem about a scientist
living between observation and intervention
a quiet witness until fledglings fall in water

I wanted to write a poem about cavity dwellers
but it became a poem about farmers
in developing nations preserving nests

I wanted to write a poem about cavity dwellers
but it became a poem about the web of connections,
it became a birdsong singing, *all my relations*

ON GROWTH
Rae Armantrout

Dressed all in plastic,
which means oil,

we're bright-eyed, scrambling
for the coloured cubes

spilled
on the rug's polymer.

Inside each
is a tiny car.

When we can't unscrew the tops
we cry for help.

We're optimists.

To sleep is to fall
into belief.

Airing even
our worst suspicions
may be pleasurable;

we are carried,
buoyed.

In sleep,
the body can heal itself,
grow larger.

Creatures that never wake
can sprout a whole new
limb,

a tail.

This may be wrong.

SPECULATIVE FICTION
Rae Armantrout

1

The idea that producing a string of nonsense syllables
while pointing toward an object
may cause that object to change
is common in children on the verge of language.

The idea that force exists only
as an interaction between objects
while an object
is a kind of kink
            in a force field.

The idea that, if one survives X number of years,
one will live to see how things 'turn out'
or even that things 'end well.'

2

In the future we will face new problems.

How will we represent the variety of human types
once all the large animals are gone?

As sly as a mother;
as hungry as an orphan?

SARAH MANGLE
@sarahmangle

Jessica Houston, *Crossing the Line*, 2015.

Jessica Houston, *The Greening*, 2015.

Aude Moreau, *The Blue Line / La ligne bleue*, 2013, maquette.

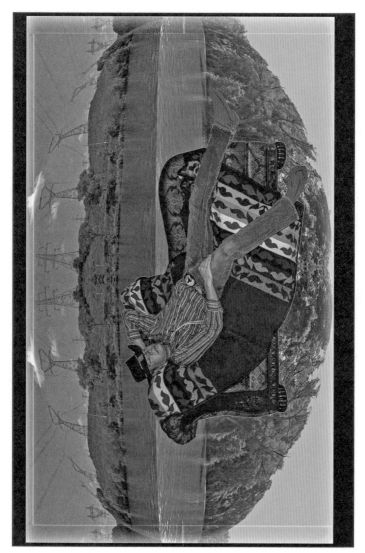

Shelley Niro, *Sleeping Warrior Dreams of Pastures and Power.*

Shelley Niro, *Sleeping Warrior, Dressing Warrior.*

RECLAIMING OUR NAMES
Waubgeshig Rice

Our son's full name is Jiikwis Dean Manoominii. There are many stories behind it, as with any name in any culture. He's lived with it for more than two and a half years now, and we all echo it proudly amongst friends, family, and strangers. He can pronounce every syllable now, which are the sweetest sounds to a parent's ears.

My wife Sarah and I put a lot of thought into his name before he arrived. It was important to us as Anishinaabeg to have his name reflect his culture, language, and family history. And as is custom in many Anishinaabe communities, we asked for help to determine what he would be called for the rest of his life. Naming him was a family affair, and we didn't want it any other way.

Shortly after we found out a child was coming to us, I offered my father *semaa* (tobacco) to find a name. Where I'm from, elders are often asked to help name children. It's a custom steeped in respect and ceremony, and we were proud to carry it forward. My grandmother named me after her father, an act that has firmly connected me to my family and community throughout my life. We wanted the same for our child.

He was born early and very traumatically. He spent his first days without a name because we weren't ready for him. As he and his mother recovered in hospital, my father and stepmother visited us. It was then we learned from my dad that our son would be called Jiikwis, a word that can mean 'first born,' 'first son,' or 'oldest brother' in Anishinaabemowin. It refers to Majiikwis, a key figure in immemorial Anishinaabe stories.

His second name, Dean, is an homage to his great-grandfather of the same name on his mother's side. She and I are both of mixed Anishinaabe and Canadian heritage, so we felt a name in English was important to include as well. Determining his last name, though, was a more significant act of reclamation.

Manoominii is a variation of the word for wild rice in the Anishinaabe language, and it's what his wild-rice-farming ancestors on my side used to be called. In the mid-nineteenth century, they were among a group of Potawatomi people who fled the territory now known as Wisconsin, forced out by the Indian Removal Act signed by U.S. President Andrew Jackson years earlier. They settled around the Great Lakes, joining people who had established long-standing Anishinaabe communities in the region.

When the Indian Act was passed in Canada in 1876, the federal government forced Indigenous people to register as 'Indians' under the state. My great-great-grandfather, known as John Menominee, was told he had to change what was considered his last name in order to do so. (Anishinaabeg didn't traditionally use last names, and how he came to be called John Menominee is unknown.)

The Canadian authorities gave him the surname Rice because it was a translation they identified for Menominee (Manoominii), and it's what that branch of my family has been known as since. Our wild-rice heritage was thus erased in name, and would only be passed down in story.

In recent decades, though, some of my relatives have reclaimed that identity. Two of my aunts legally changed Rice back to Menominee, and one of my uncles registered his children with that last name at birth. That inspired us to do the same for Jiikwis, using a more modern spelling according to the now widely adopted double-vowel system. And it was fairly easy to do.

When we registered his birth online through Service Ontario, we had the option to give him a different last name. It was as simple as selecting an option from a drop-down menu and typing 'Manoominii' into a box. There was no additional cost, and his birth certificate arrived shortly after with his name spelled out as such, for as long as he decides to carry it.

He'll know the stories of his names as he grows up. Hopefully, he'll be proud of them. But he'll be very aware of the history of his people, and how colonialism has attempted to tear down and erase their identity. Just speaking his name is an act of resistance and reclamation. They're words and stories the settler authorities didn't want spoken on this land any longer. Yet here they are, echoing for generations to come.

WHETHER THE HEAVENS BREAK
Margaret Christakos

WHETHER THE HEAVENS BREAK

WHETHER THE BROKEN CLOUDS ACCUMULATE
    ENOUGH AUDIENCE TO DEBUT AT TIFF

WHETHER CURIOUS CUMULI INCUBATE OUR ATTENTION

WHETHER THE WEATHER BURSTS FORTH
    LIKE HEAVEN'S GATES LOCKING DOWN
    ALL THE LATCHES

WHETHER WATER AND ETHER COMBINED
    MAKE A BEAUTIFUL SUNSET

WHETHER DUSK IS UPON US SOONER
    RATHER THAN LATER

WHETHER YOU PREFER HURRICANES OVER HEAT WAVES
    MONSOONS OVER ICE MELTS

WHETHER YOU HARVEST FRUIT FROM THE FOREST FLOOR
    OR WITHERED ON WIZENED VINES

WHETHER YOU PINE FOR YOUR MUSKOKA CHILDHOOD

WHETHER PILEATED WOODPECKERS DELIGHT YOU

EITHER THE CONTINUOUS PRESENT OR
    THE LOOMING FUTURE

EITHER SOME OF THEM OR ALL OF US

WHETHER EMPATHY

WHETHER MORALITY

WHETHER TRUTH WAVERS BEFORE SIX-DOLLAR LATTES
    AND MAUVE MACARONS

WHETHER IT WAS A TOTAL BLOCKBUSTER

WHETHER YOU'VE NEVER SEEN ANYTHING LIKE IT

WHETHER THE SKY GETS DARKER THAN *BREAKING BAD*

WHETHER REALITY IS A MALEVOLENT COLOSSUS

    COMING ON LIKE AN ADORABLE BABY LION

WHETHER SUPER-WINDSTORMS MAKE THE RATINGS RISE

WHETHER THE DEADLINE PREMIERE

    IS A NO-HOLDS-BARRED DOCUMENTARY ON

    SUBLIME SUB-SAHARAN DROUGHT

DO WE HAVE OUR TICKET IN ADVANCE

DO WE HAVE OUR SEAT RESERVED

DO WE HAVE A COVETED SPOT BESIDE THE RED CARPET

WHETHER WE LIKE COMEDIES

    OR THRENODIES

WHETHER THE FILMMAKER WAS FUNDED

    BY A FRACKING CONGLOMERATE OR A BRAZILIAN

    MINING CONSORTIUM

WHETHER THE CLIMAX IS A MASS-SHOOTING EVENT

    THAT SOUNDED LIKE A RUNAWAY TRAIN

    THAT BARRELLED INTO CANADIAN TIRE

    LIKE A BLOOD AVALANCHE AT NIAGARA

WE'VE NEVER SEEN ANYTHING LIKE IT BEFORE

STEP RIGHT THIS WAY

STEP INTO THE HARSH GLARE

    OF THE BIGGEST SHOW ON EARTH

WHETHER WHATEVER WE DREAM

    IS JUST LIKE A MOVIE

WHETHER IT IS ALL JUST LIKE CUTTING-EDGE CINEMA

WHETHER WE'RE ON 24/7 CANDID CAMERA

ALONG WITH FACIAL RECOGNITION HOW ABOUT

    GLACIAL RECOGNITION OR WILL THAT

    SPOIL THE PLOTLINE FOR US

WHETHER IT IS ALL SO ORIGINAL

WHETHER IT IS CRAZY GENIUS AT HAND

      WHEN THE HEAVENS HEAVE AND THREATEN

YES   THE SKY MIGHT BREAK OPEN

YES   THE SKY IS MADE OF GOSSAMER ETHER

YES   ETHER IS MADE OF TRANSHUMAN MEMORY

YES   THE MEMORY DRINKS IN RAIN

YES   THE AUDIENCE IS AN OCEAN

WE WANT THE C.G.A. WEATHER TO LOOK

      MORE WILD THAN WILDERNESS ALONE

WE WANT THE ENDING TO SHOCK US

WE WANT TO BE AWAKE

SO WAKE UP

CAN WE WAKE UP

LET'S WAKE UP

FOR THE FERAL SPLENDOUR THAT REMAINS

CAConrad

for Kazim Ali

sometimes I strain
to hear one
natural
sound
when gender blurs in a
poem my world sets a
tooth in the gear
if god is in me
when will I ask for
my needs to be met
every god is qualified
it is not such a secret
when I was afraid of the
road I learned to drive
map says name of
your city in ocean
line drawn to it
towing behind
the big party
history of life on
earth might be
interesting to a
visitor one day
chewing parsley and
cilantro together is for
me where forest
meets meadow
in a future life
would we like to

fall in love with the
world as it is with
no recollection
of the beauty
we destroy
today

ALTERED AFTER TOO MANY YEARS UNDER THE MASK
CAConrad

I feel you
judging me for
becoming agoraphobic
in someone else's house
I forget how I learned to stroll through
grocery stores as though there is no crisis
my elbow cannot touch the middle of my back
my fingers though have found every part of me
soon no migration of wild animals will
be unknown to humans we will chart
film record publish archive everything
it gives us something to do while we
annihilate beauty poets shovelling
a quarry that is really an ongoing
crime scene investigation
a study in vomit imitating
vast chronicles of the face
whatever world we can hold
we will never agree our
neglect was worth it
whatever amount of
crazy we can imagine
coming at us double it
I found the perfect
listening chair nothing
but listeners who sit
I am sitting in it now
listening to my friend
the photographer
whose self-portrait

I find reflected
in eyes
of her
every
photo

HALFLING BEAR (ECLIPSE)
Joanne Arnott

the trophy hunter has it
the scientists & the media
celebrate, debate, discuss
photos of the corpse fly
all around the world
& linger for years

the miracle of courtship
alignment sought & found
the passing of a honeymoon
the wonder of apparent difference
transcended with pleasure

the private rendezvous of
polar bear & grizzly, followed
by months of solitary gestation
of nurturing, nursing
feeding
teaching the young

all the years of a young bear's life
discoveries, missteps, accomplishments
the cultural patterning inhabited, as
taught by the mother
& the world met, step by step

all these
disappear

into bloodlust & big money
dna proofs & a too small sample
the death of a halfling bear reveals
the minds of scientific observers
& all forms of prejudice: miscegenation
still, so scandalous

this is not a freakshow
but evidence of life unfolding
& showing its shape as it goes,
the elders say, *usually they fight*
but not this time

AS LONG AS
Nicole Brossard

it swings in the face smells
as a cloud falling on the skin
yes my dear body of spoken and written words
it crashes in the ear, the mouth,
life everlasting until
les catastrophes d'eau, le shining
until the mind wants to
lick again that slow taste of civilization

fifty-six glaciers gone in ten years
someone spoke about a frightened nation and asked
where *lac* hides in glacier and placenta
then an author wrote a book about the encounter of
of grandmothers, glaciers, holy cows, and
a quick melt of mythologies,
then I had to translate and move into another sentence
au milieu du chaos nous sortons nos couteaux

SOFT BODY TIDALECTICS
Whitney French

Ocean asks to save this:
this transition
to the next world
in a wave,

prying the gates
from one realm to the next
open.

an open sore on Ocean's
lip, our finite bodies split
raw & salted,
return to the sea.

islanders' whole lives:
a delicate balance
between coast & cove.

noses flare
as salt fills our lungs,
as crisping palm leaves
twisting in sand
and the sound of bare feet
scrambling up hillside:
one, two many
mud slides
wash away our homes.

flotsam does as it always does;
gurgling along the cresting waves,

the shore bleeds
and knows no line

yet the way coastal erosion
holds our secrets, how deep
reef vegetation sits
                    suspended
between sea-surface
& sea-floor,
it's as if it calls us
back to our true Selves;
the blue pushes us up against a new portal
our ancestral back and fro.

those who endure, watch!
as tides conspire
to hold even the dead
accountable.

memory,
she rivers in the body,
caught up in her own
rush, in a wave
to the next world

this transition, Ocean asks
to save this.

YOU SAY YOU HEAR US AND THAT YOU UNDERSTAND THE URGENCY
Jessica Le

The year is unknown and we are running
through alleyways. Again and again, we pass
by poster ads for strangely shaped watermelon,
Get it in a square! Get it in a triangle! Hell, get it
in whatever shape you like. They drip red paint
onto the ground. Lives spent chasing and being chased,
breaking into houses already broken
into – green-leaf wrath and choking. Behind the
ivy we make fun of graffiti-covered walls, turning weather warnings
into dance numbers, and in the background there is always
the record playing on repeat: It's not too late. It's not
too late. It's not too late. So by the time we make it
to the dust street, clambering onto the top of the car,
it's nearly dawn. We're taking in the prairie, arms extended,
wondering if the dove will come down
on its own or if it needs to be beckoned.

Title from Greta Thunberg's speech at the UN Climate Action Summit on
September 23, 2019.

I NEVER GOT OVER SIXTY LIKES
Kirby

O darlins
when hasn't life been expendable?
Another train departs
tossed on a heap of disposables
Cell phones   plastics   mountains
There is no law
only the monied
This too shall pass
We already know the ending
We've seen it
left before the credits
Just   one   click
In a darkened theatre
'Why did you unfollow me?'
'You unfriended me bitch'
The price of the ticket
to see what might happen
Any surprises   plot twists
shot in glorious black and white
Light projected   a fresh stream
the cup of one's hands
When there was free water to drink
'Can I have a glass of water?'
'Water   some water   please'
You only think you're tired
The entire sick fucking world is
tired of this   all of this
Maybe I'll text Christopher
see if they're tired, too.

THE HEART IS A KNOT
Chris Bailey

my father says, *and the heart is the softest part*
of the hardwood. It's so close to rot.

We are tacking in oak lath for the bottoms of lobster traps.

Not a light tap, no gentle touch in the building

drug home from the harbour on wooden skids,
hauled with thick chains by a tractor that sits

outside the doors waiting for snow to settle.
Find nailhead with the hammer's face. Drive

the thing home. Let your hand be heavy
like the weight of February cold. The wind

with so much north in it, the shores shift.
The mouth of the harbour sands over now

every year. The jut of land between North Lake
and East Point gone, like the good oak for traps

gone for the floors of large houses that sit
empty three quarters of the year. Part-time residents

who want full-time say over taxes,
pavement, over windmills that churn

Island air their lungs seldom breathe.
My father says, *You'd get junks of cod*

come in the traps like this.
How far apart he holds his hands.

And now. He stops, shakes his head.
Points to the laths I've driven in.

gLITTER
Karen Lee

we bedazzle faces
praise galaxies
night binds durags
glitter-greased hair
rippled edges

gentle microbeads
scour alter egos
(or chickpea flour
turmeric   ground
flaxseed)

repeat
rinse gilt in living Wata

faces fill oceans
slick fish nip glitter
how can they
with three eyes   not?
lifeless microplastics
rush open mouths

seafood litters
glow-in-the-dark
bodies   Ocean trash
glares veins

stuffed with glitter
cupcakes   chocolate
lattes   beer   gold

prosecco roast chicken
   (beg yuh oxtail   curry
   goat   peanut stew
   please)
slow-baked   festive
suicide on scintillating
invites

Wata darkens   scarce
where Indigenous   Black
Brown   downpressed
thrive
opacity saturates refuse

hush!
drink fluoride Wata
drool antidepressants
pharmaceutical glaze
soothes chaos

hot air pins planets
in place   glitter
crowds bird bellies

stars   earth   sea life
pity our glitter-lit blood
gilt hearts   glossed
fossils beat

they will say

post-apocalyptic
   intergalactic
   greenhouse

glitterstorm
fart of fractal
reflections

Sirius::
the beautiful
ones have gone

Mother Earth::
what in the cluster
fuck?!?!?

Mami-Wata::
who nuh hear
wi feel

cockroaches::
but what a way
dem did pretty

THE LARGER FORGETTING
Laurie D. Graham

Stone barn, fuel cloud, chipmunk, dump truck,
dry rustle, goldenrod, milkweed, raspberry –

springing to life each morning ahistorical,
into excess of obliterated lot, deciphering

food on store shelves, lighting fires
that smoke from what's burning,

dismantling any tree, any squirm
of consciousness within one's human field –

fire hydrant, manure flinger, diesel smell,
man under tall cap disking silty loam,

ducks across the storm pond,
snowmobile path, tractor path –

one day stripped to clay and laced with streets
named for British lieutenants

or for what's been dozed away –

walking trail, chain link, fence board,
walk-out basement, facades of stone,

corn stalks, wet clay, crow call, asphalt crumble –
engines unrelenting across our horizons,

a minor second where the original
was a different mode entirely –

garden of scalloped concrete pads,
a weed whacker through crabgrass,

the dips of the driveways, the barbecue covers,
the back-alley cigarette butts –

a digger ripping up a structure,
yanking plumbing and support beams,

balanced on a carpet of limestone bricks,
on a carpet of river stones,

flag taped to digger's window,
brown seeds in silk through the demo site,

cement truck turning, set back from the action,
and the butterflies move differently,

in the shape of a question, hooking off
in another direction once the asking's done –

concrete washout, standing water,
AC units, parking structures,

workers' phobic dollar-store pranks,
rigs, busted streetlights, a loud wailing,

expletives thrown in the face of a panhandler,
wheat-paste advertising, landscapers, tar spillage,

tree sentences, place making,
high, deep gusts today, dread –

RHAPSODIC TRIP
Jen Currin

We tripped the CEO –
he was late and bruised
to the meeting.
Yet they can't be classified as 'terrorists,'
seeing as we never see them
outside a suit or a boardroom
where they detonate suicide belts
and rise in smoke
to form another corporation
out at sea, beyond the spills,
riding to their islands
on oily dolphins.

Here in the city, good company
of thieves and skaters, bicyclists
believing in microbrew.

Someone down the block without a watch
building a stone wall
in the rain
asks the time.

Wake o'clock, brother.

TO PLANT LIFE (ALL)
Francine Cunningham

you show what you heal
in your very makeup,
the cellular structure of what you are
giving us a map to all it means to be alive

seen in valerian root
shaped like a nervous system,
used to calm our nerves
and send us to sleep

seen in strawberries
cut in half,
the picture of a human heart,
used to heal our hearts

seen in St. John's wort
bright yellow flowers
calling forth joy,
used to heal depression

you show us and
sadly, only some of us see

GREY WATER
Carleigh Baker

The ocean is still this morning, and I can't even tell you what a relief that is. Those waves have been pounding away for days, maybe weeks, who the hell knows? Drowning out every thought, every sound. Those MP3 files you sent? Couldn't hear them. Tried to sit outside and listen, sun on my face, smashed remnants of a crab shell gathering flies beside me, but I got only the faintest inkling of your voice, the slightest rhythm of your poems. New poems! You're so prolific.

Who knows where my earbuds are. At the bottom of an unpacked box somewhere. I was holding the laptop up to my ear until thoughts of brain cancer washed away all other attempts at concentration. On your voice. That's what I really wanted to hear. Finally I gave up on the romantic image of listening to you read poems while I gazed at the ocean and went inside. But I can hear the waves inside, too, just enough to bug me. Finally I got in the closet, laptop pressed against my ear again (screw cancer!) and could just make out your dulcet tones. Something about a train. And bugs. And sex, I think, though it's so hard to tell with you. Those fancy metaphors. At one point you mentioned trying to capture the (non-sexy) simplicity of an afternoon of mid-summer rain. What I wouldn't give for some rain right now. Amanda says the well could dry up at any time, and then what?

Amanda is a pain, even when she's not here. She texts every day, asking if it's rained yet. Like she couldn't just google it. She wants me to take three-minute showers to conserve water, but it's hard to wash everything in three minutes. Impossible, really. I do upper body on Monday and Friday and lower body on Wednesday and Saturday. That includes hair washing for upper body and leg shaving for lower body, and as you know I have very long hair and legs. Damn, that didn't sound as sexy as I wanted it to. Anyway, yeah, two showers in a row on weekends. You never know when you might get lucky – not that I'm looking – but hopefully it'd be on a Saturday, when my hair is reasonably clean and my legs are baby smooth. You'd like me on Saturday. You'd take the 5:20 ferry over, and walk from the terminal to the bookstore, and I'd pretend to be a little surprised that it was already 6:30, even though I'd have been waiting the whole day. We'd go to the pizza place after work and have a couple glasses of wine and an appy outside on the patio.

I'd have my nerd glasses on and my day-old hair up in a bun, kind of like a sexy librarian, only like a sexy bookseller. That's me. We'd leave the pizza place before it got too dark, since it's a long walk to the pub. Maybe I'll get a car someday. Somebody might pick us up, a good-hearted local, somebody I served at the bookstore that day. If not, we'd take the path that runs alongside the road. It's fine during the day, but a little too creepy at night. There are no predators on the island. Just deer and raccoons. A local told me that the deer might take a run at me during rutting season but he might have been joking. Most of the time they're just running away. Or sometimes they hang out in the backyard and watch me, big watery Bambi eyes, tails twitching. Anyway, we might see some deer on the way to the pub. When we arrived, some islanders would be smoking a doobie outside, off in the trees a little. Neither of us would feel uncomfortable – it's the island!

I'd know the bartender, and he'd bring my martini over and shake your hand and ask you what you'd like. You'd be a little suspicious of how well he and I seem to know each other, and I'd reassure you that although he's quite handsome, and he does have a way with words, he's not my type. You are. There'd be a reggae band playing, and you'd remark that reggae seems appropriate for the island. You'd be right.

At one point you'd pull something you'd written on the ferry out of your pocket and read it to me: a new poem or piece of flash fiction, or an excerpt from a novel in progress. I'd listen rapturously, chin cradled between my fingers, running my foot up and down your leg under the table. You wouldn't even stop to thank the bartender when he brought your beer, you'd be so into it. The bartender would nod approvingly and wink at me. Because we're friends, and I've told him all about you. And you're every bit as good in person as in my stories.

We'd have too many beers, and dance to the reggae band and whatever the DJ was playing afterwards, and we'd even end up outside smoking some weed with the locals before you'd wrap your arms around me and say, 'Let's go home,' and I'd say, 'It's a thirty-minute walk,' and you'd say, 'I'll piggyback you.'

And you would.

Damn.

It's probably not a great idea to do this to myself – imagine you here like this. It's comforting for a while, but it doesn't take long before I really start to feel sad. Making new friends isn't easy. I spend most days here at Amanda's house, reading, drinking wine. And looking across the Salish Sea at the ferry terminal in Tsawwassen. And wishing I could take a bath, which might seem like a strange thing to crave in this heat. Obviously, in a world of three-minute showers, baths are way, way out. Non-negotiable. And yet here I am, back from an hour-long walk home, hunched over my laptop, writing you, and looking across the hall at the tub. No friendly local stopped to offer me a ride. You weren't here to piggyback me. You're probably reading de Maupassant in a coffee shop on Commercial Drive, or something like that. *It is the lives we encounter that make life worth living.* De Maupassant said that. You're across the Salish Sea. I am here. It's harder to be here than you think. I know you said I looked relaxed last time we Skyped. I have to tell you a secret.

I was relaxed last time we Skyped. Because I'd had a bath. I know, I know! But it wasn't just a whim, I'd had a terrible day: yelling customers, screaming kids, a nasty pain behind my right eye that flared with every blink. When I got home, I dropped my laptop on the ground and smashed the corner of the LCD screen, cracked it, and that was just the last straw. I fell down on my knees and cried. Partly about the laptop and partly about my knees. Amanda has stone floors. I know that sounds melodramatic, but you don't know how stressful it's been. I was desperate to move home, to be with you. Since you refuse to come here to be with me.

I cried until there were no more tears, and then I poured myself a glass of wine. I sat out in the backyard, facing those bloody waves that never seem to stop smashing at the cliff, and one glass of wine turned into three. Those goddamn waves! I wanted still water, warm water. I wanted comfort. So I stomped upstairs and I did it. I drew a bath.

The well water has a lot of sulphur in it, so the bathroom smelled pretty rank, but Amanda's scented candles helped. I closed all the windows and put my poor, cracked laptop on the side of the tub and queued up all of the MP3s you've sent. The suite of poems, the novel excerpts, the seventy-five flash fiction stories based on *À la recherche du temps perdu* (which I've listened to dozens of times and really connect with, even though I've never read any Proust). You're so much smarter than me, so much more well read. The candles smelled like cinnamon and cranberry, the water was steaming, and your voice was so buttery. When I shrugged off my bathrobe, a shiver of goose-flesh washed over me. My nipples hardened to buds. I imagined you standing there behind me, extending a hand to help me into the water. Your eyes on my body as it disappeared into the bubbles. I sat back, piling my hair up and tying it with an elastic, though some tendrils escaped and brushed my shoulders. You could have sat on the toilet and rubbed my feet, and recited all seventy-five stories. That's what I imagined, anyway. The cover of a romance novel, or an Amy Winehouse music video.

Wouldn't that be nice?

I sat in the water until it was nearly cold, to make sure I got the most use out of it. Surely no one could begrudge me one bath! Amanda that jerk, off frolicking in Iceland with some guy for the summer, all those beautiful blue volcanic hot springs, all the sulphury hot water in the world.

But I'll tell you something else, and this I'm particularly proud of. I saved all the grey water – that's what you call it after you've soaked in it, in case you didn't know – and I used it to do things like water the dahlias in the garden, which Amanda has actually insisted I do, even though I'm supposed to be limiting myself to three-minute showers. Doesn't that seem kind of weird to you? Don't worry about yourself, but make sure a bunch of decorative plants in the front yard look their best. Make sure they get enough water. *The dahlias are more important than you.* That's kind of what she's saying, right? A bunch of goddamn flowers! I wasn't sure where Amanda keeps her buckets, so I used a bowl, which meant taking many trips up and down the stairs, but what else is there to do with all this time to myself? I've used about half the water in the tub, so the rest is still sitting there. When it's gone, I'll reward myself with another bath.

Your letter hasn't arrived yet. I know it takes you awhile to write them, since you insist on using that complex pen and ink cursive. It's beautiful. The letters are masterpieces: exercises in shape and form, gentle thoughts, flowing words. But it takes forever, and sometimes I wish you'd apply the same quantity-over-quality value to personal interaction that you have for flash fiction. No offence, the quality of the flash fiction is still very high. I read a Buzzfeed article that said introverts have no time for small talk. But small talk has a purpose sometimes. It fills in the cracks between people. Maybe I'll get your letter tomorrow and feel bad for sniping at you. I'm sorry. It takes mail extra long to get to the island, of course. Everything here is slower and more expensive. I thought the slower part would be nice. But damn, we're talking *really* slow.

Amanda called to check on the dahlias, can you believe that? She didn't ask how I was doing. The dahlias are fine, and the herbs are spectacular, they love a good drought. I was so annoyed at her when I got off the phone I decided to have another bath. But there was still some grey water left in the tub, not much, about two inches. I sponged out a little, into the stainless steel bowls, but then I gave up and just ran the damn water. Baths aren't really the cleanest endeavour anyway. Sitting in your own filth, sloughed skin, bacteria. I noticed that the sides of the tub were a little crusty, so I decided I'd completely empty it and clean it out after the bath. But I was so relaxed when I got out, I lay down on the bed and fell asleep. Now it's morning, and the water has been sitting in there all night, and I'm feeling really guilty. I'll take a bunch downstairs to the garden. It's Monday, upper-body day. Which is good, because my hair is kind of gross after soaking in the tub. I should have tied it up. Not like there's anyone here to notice.

You know, I've seen photos of the drought situation in California. Comparison between now and ten years ago: reservoirs, riverbeds, lakes. Have you seen the photos? The situation looks pretty grim. But last time we visited, I remember people watering their lawns, boulevards with lush green grass, the long, long shower we took together the morning before we left. All the swimming pools we passed over on our flight home, little blue tiles crammed into an uncomfortable crush of stucco and asphalt. Water is everything, and they don't have much. Neither do we. The boulevards in Vancouver were green when I left. Are they still? Don't you feel guilty every time you take a drink?

❧

You're not going to believe what happened. You won't believe it, you'll think I'm making it up, but I'm not, I swear. Yesterday when I got home from work, water was flowing from the ceiling. At first I didn't realize that it was coming from above. I thought the bottled water dispenser was leaking when I realized my feet were wet, but then I looked up. Drip drip drip. The walls were soaked, and get this, the light fixtures were full. Bulbs encased in little frosted glass fish bowls. Can you imagine if I'd turned on the lights?

Well, you know what I thought, of course. The bathtub. I never did get around to cleaning it, so it's still about three-quarters full. I thought maybe the weight had caused some kind of catastrophe upstairs. I slipped and bashed my knee on the way up, but I was so scared I barely noticed. My bathroom was fine though. So I ran over to Amanda's bathroom and the toilet was leaking! I've never even used that toilet! I had no idea what to do, so I went back downstairs and put pots under the worst spots, pulled towels out of the linen closet and wadded them up around the pots. I just kept thinking, 'this could be used for the dahlias!' I went back up to the upstairs toilet and noticed that it was just running constantly, and I remembered something about jiggling the handle when that happens (I think it's in a Tom Waits song, right? 'And the toilet's running, aww christ, shake the handle.' Right? Am I losing it?). So that's what I did. Then I turned off the valves behind the toilet and that stopped the flooding part, but I still had to spend all evening mopping up the house, emptying the pots and wringing the towels out, outside in the garden of course. I wish it would fucking rain.

If you were here tonight, I'd light a fire in the wood stove. I know it's still too warm for fires. We'd open all the windows and doors. The sea would be still. Even with the night's breeze, it'd be sweltering, ridiculous to have a fire, so we'd get naked and lay on the cool stone floor. Any skin contact would be so uncomfortable, but you'd leave your hand on my belly, slick sweat bonding us, sticky drips pooling below the arch of my back. Every so often, I'd mop it up.

I think the overflowing toilet was a sign. I know it was. I've been wasteful, terribly, terribly wasteful. Like you, in Vancouver. You have boulevards, I have baths. We are terrible. I came to the island to write, and I haven't written a word, except to you. And you haven't written back. We don't actually care how things will turn out, do we? What's going to happen when the earth runs dry?

↯

'I vant to be alone. I just vaaaant to be alone.' Like Greta Garbo from that movie; what's the one? *Grand Hotel.* I've got a two-minute YouTube clip here. Garbo's keepers speaking desperately on the phone, looking for our heroine. Then, she suddenly appears in the foreground, tussled, a picture of malaise. The other characters – a concerned-looking matron and a grim, fatherly man – approach Garbo.

'Where've you been?' he demands.

And then Garbo says it. Breathes it. *I vant to be aloooone.* That's where the clip ends.

The island is long and skinny, and most houses are set away from the road, down long driveways. As a result, the roads seem empty. It's like the world just petered out quietly, no bombs, no zombies. Dry ferns along the shoulder, droopy evergreens, dry creek beds harbouring empty cigarette packages and yogurt containers. There's still the deer, I told you about them.

Sometimes, if I look at a deer for too long, I get weepy.

It still hasn't rained, but it's starting to cool off. Last week, on a misty road that was presenting me with a seriously pastoral farm landscape, I saw a snake. Just a garter snake, no big deal. I used to catch garters when I was a kid and freak the boys out with them. I loved the feel as they hugged my wrist, coiling themselves around it like they were claiming me.

I slowed down, but as I got closer, I saw it was half-squashed. There was more carnage further along – a couple of flat lizards. The road was a reptile deathtrap. I looked away, at the horses in the fields, dehydrated green beans hanging from a lattice, sun diffusing onto Scotch broom. A foreign plant, and invasive, one of the locals told me. Still, it's pretty. I tried to take a photo to send you, but I couldn't do it justice. So I kept walking.

And then, yesterday, an eagle flew overhead and dropped a lizard on the ground right in front of me – yes, dropped it! – and it was still alive. Alive, but stunned. It was frozen in place on the road in front of me. Staring. I ran a finger across its mottled brown skin and it didn't move. I pulled out my phone and took a picture, not often you get the opportunity for such a closeup. But then I got worried. If it stayed put, eventually somebody was going to run it over. So I picked it up by the tail, crouching low to the ground in case it wiggled out of my grasp and fell again, but it didn't. I walked a long way into the woods, until I found a soft bed of moss – vibrant green and threaded with thin orange tendrils. There were a couple of clusters of unremarkable beige mushrooms growing nearby, and I could hear the gurgle of a stream, which was pretty amazing, since it still hasn't rained. I couldn't figure out how this place had avoided the drought; maybe an underground spring? But it seemed like a really nice place for a lizard to be. I took another photo, and when I looked at my phone, I realized that its skin wasn't brown, but quite a dramatic shade of purple. How had I not seen that? Maybe it changed when I put it on the moss?

I looked back down at the little guy, still suspended in time, and wondered if he really was still alive. Maybe he was dead. Maybe he was a she. Maybe something both otherworldly and organic was reaching out to me, trying to give me a message, and I was slapping its hands away like an idiot. Something magic. There have been other moments: eagles startled from cliffs, unexplained rock pilings. A tree with a big white equal sign painted on it, which was clearly a message to veer off the road and into the bushes. Before long I had bushwhacked my way into a grassy field. When I arrived (I can't explain how I knew that I'd arrived, at a certain point I just stopped walking) the first thing I felt was fear. Like I'd come to a sinister place, something out of a horror film. Like some guy in a hockey mask was waiting. But that instinct was wrong, not an instinct at all, really. Maybe the opposite of an instinct. A powerful and lifelong misconception that I am not a part of nature. After I stood there for a while, I wanted to sing, I really wanted to sing, and even though I was worried someone might hear and think I was crazy, I suspected that that, too, was a powerful and lifelong misconception. Nobody is ever really paying attention to anyone but themselves. So I sang. I didn't have any real words to sing, but I'd been listening to some pretty schmaltzy New Age music that morning, so I sang that. The whole thing may have been schmaltzy, but when the tiny songbirds started to sing along with me, I admit, it felt like a prayer.

Make no mistake, this place is magic. But magic can overwhelm you, it can make you sick. Disoriented. Twice now I've walked up to the bluffs on crisp mornings (still no rain) and looked out on Active Pass. There are other islands out there, which makes me feel better. Twice I've been overcome by gratitude for what the island is trying to give me – this new and complex perspective – and I've thanked it. And twice, at that very moment, I've heard the watery exhale of a whale. Surely such a thing should convince me of my place here, of my connection to the land. But it doesn't, and I think it's because you're not here. I leave the bluffs wondering if I've imagined the whole thing, if I'm losing it. Why can't we believe in these serendipitous moments with nature, or maybe even that nature might want to communicate with us? That it is constantly in communication with us. Lord knows we believe all kinds of other crazy shit.

⚘

You're going to think this is nuts. That is, IF you're still reading anything I'm sending you. I don't care. I've been thinking about those fucking dahlias, and you in the city with those big boulevards – big, useless boulevards – and I think, *that's not what water is for.* Not for keeping something so grotesquely unnecessary alive. Something that is constantly dying. Well, I guess we can't do anything about the dying part, we're *all* constantly dying, but some things are certainly more worthy of life than others. Dahlias are not worthy; they are big and showy and unnatural. Their heads grow so big, they'll fall right over if you don't tie them up. That's it, they actually grow themselves to death. But what about frogs? Eelgrass. Algae and moss and mould. Lichens!

Delicate things are suffering. I found three dead lizards around a dusty depression in the forest where there used to be a pond. They're desperate. I went looking for the spring I found a few weeks ago, no luck. But I've got space for them! The well's still not dry – I'm still the beneficiary of its gift, stagnant and sulphur-ish as it may be. And it's pretty bad. Amanda actually told me to bring home more of the bottled water we get delivered to the bookstore so I could avoid using the taps completely. I did bring some back, but I decided they'd do more good in the bathtub, where I've started something wonderful.

An ecosystem!

If you were here, I'd show you everything. The bio filter: bacteria, protozoa, and phytoplankton. You wouldn't be able to see those guys, of course, not without a microscope. Did you know that even though protozoa are single cells, some of them exhibit animal-like behaviour? Though they're not considered primitive animals, not anymore. But some of them hunt like predators, totally badass, I read it on Wikipedia. Anyway, I'm sure they're in there. Then there's the zooplankton. They are definitely animals – tiny and delicate. I'm not sure if I have any zooplankton yet – as you can imagine, it's hard to find lake water, and anything from the ocean would die in the tub. I'm thinking of ordering something online, from an aquarium supply store. And then there are the snails (these were really hard to find but worth it). The frogs were easy to find but hard to catch. Now they're hard to keep confined to the tub; every time I open the bathroom door one or two jump out and I have to chase them down the hall. Rough-skinned newts, that's who I'm looking for next, same as the guy that eagle dropped. Clearly that was a sign. And the leaking toilet. I see the connections now. You're probably shaking your head at this, but you haven't been here. With every day so quiet and clear, things start to work themselves out.

I'd work on the moss garden. You'd tend to the worms and insects with such care and attention, and together we'd foster the nitrogen cycle: waste to ammonia, to nitrates, to nutrition, to waste. Beautiful life, safe from everything, inside. It's small, of course. Just a bathtub. But once we got some fish in there, we'd have a humble food source. As soon as the rain started again, we'd never have to leave.

THE WORLD ENDS FOR GOOD THIS TIME
Manahil Bandukwala

First it was winter and
winter refused to end. The solstice came, then

the equinox, but days
did not cool, they did not
give precious extra minutes
of light. Just clouds

and clouds greyed sidewalks for months.
Then it was summer

and summer did not end. We celebrated
its stay but we should
not have. The leaves turned
yellow and that
should have been
our sign

but an extra day, an extra few
precious hours
at the end
of the world. We basked
in it as we marched

with our signs, sipped
iced coffee when we should
have wrapped
our hands up in wool. The summer

ends late but winter
comes early and this
is what we give, a snow-covered field.
The world ends in white
and solar flares. It is when

we do away with the in-betweens,
the equilibriums
of red leaves and flower buds
of rain rain rain,

find ourselves huddled together
in a corner cafe
on carpets and couches,

find a way back
to the physicality
of each other.

POTATOES
Mercedes Eng

my yt grandma once asked me 'who do you think you are, the Queen of Sheba?' why yes yt grandma I do believe I'm a hawt biblical queen of colour wreaking havoc and generally causing a ruckus because unlike you I dreamed beyond this town this river valley this province this nation state this gender

but it's not all her fault she was constantly reminding me not to get too big for my britches because she was born and raised in a time when women didn't wear pants, like, she didn't wear pants until her seventies and I don't remember her in a dress after my mom got her to try pants. my yt grandma was someone you'd want around when the apocalypse that yt people keep making movies about gets here, although the apocalypse is already here. you'd want her around because for decades she grew all the food she ate except sugar, coffee, and flour. planted seeds, tended plants, ate of the harvest. since she was in single digits, helping her fam in the fields, bragged by her father to be 'strong as an ox.' I haven't contributed to the growing of food that I eat since I was a child and when I did it was with my yt grandma.

Sarah Pereux, *The Canada Goose*, 2019, graphite on paper, 11" x 15".

Sarah Pereux, 'Trinity' from *Pretty Paws* series, 2019, graphite on paper, 5" x 7".

FLOTSAM
Sheniz Janmohamed

Bottles, plastic bags, underwear, gum wrappers,
receipts, caps, toothbrushes, lighters, cups

end up in the sea's vast net of light,
waves heaving the weight of
our waste back and forth
back and forth.

The ocean,
tumbling shards of beer bottles
into oblong pebbles of sea glass,
weaving bloated plastic bags
into nooses for seagulls,
breaking bottle caps
into bait for lantern fish.

Our sparkling garbage dump
brims with cockles and crap.

Our hands throw
trash overboard,

the giver of life receives.

LANTERN LETTER: A ZUIHITSU
Ching-In Chen

My people – I see you across street, porch people, huddled under brick archway, watching what pours from sky. Wading in water, what circuits it carries – mostly numb, small, what might feel like circuit's end.

Stay home, watch streets filling up & draining & filling up again, my neighbour with no shoes & an umbrella knock on doors to locate whose car in the street flooding up. He knocked on our door (and another one – fleeting back – knocked a few minutes before), and said, *Hi, I'm your neighbour.*

We miss what's been paved over, all branches holding down our dirt, keeping paths flowing away.

A lake in library parking lot. Women calling to each other over and above it, heading to their free computer classes. My people of the flashing lights, pulsating throbs. Carbon monoxide, methane, oxides of nitrogen. Cousins released 180,565 up into stream, 287,453 emissions. These are among us too, carried into our stories 'if we would have only sung to find each other. Or taught ourselves to read the waves.'

If only grown-resistant skin, hard-fired to stand through ravenous beetles stripping off all trees, thirty-three trillion gallons. What slugs, what acoustic activities swallowed and sat, stared down, with glass eyes.

Vow to share our four teaspoons of coffee, open backdoor at your knock, lend the orange cords, handheld pumps, small towels to slick off oil anomalies, watch for rising sheen in horizon, melting glacier, to remember its full and terrible man-eating weight, to walk through rain down boulders singing lines of poetry to the bears, announcing *hey hey we are here, don't worry, nothing to see, nothing to eat.*

If I see you coming, I vow to slow down, walk step beside you, not leave you wading through sluck, not leave you stacked chairs-high for rescue. 'Hundreds climbed silent up the highways, looking for more silence.' I'm done with fleeing. Even as you walked beside me, I feared your ever-growing branches would wild out my own tin. I kept saying, *thank you, nice to pass and cross,* and leave-taking. You waited for me, the only two large clumsies under a finally darkening midnight sky, saying *hello again, hello.*

I vow an impossible hello.

Quoted words from Alexis Pauline Gumbs' *M Archive: After the End of the World* (Duke University Press, 2018).

THE POPLAR VOTE
Kazim Ali

In 1975, Kazim Ali's family, then new immigrants to Canada, moved from Winnipeg, Manitoba, north to Jenpeg, a town built by Manitoba Hydro for its employees to live in while constructing the Jenpeg Generating Station, a dam across the Nelson River that provides electricity to the rest of the province. Forty years later, after a suicide epidemic among young people struck the Pimicikamak community of Cross Lake, upon whose land the dam is built, Kazim Ali returned north at the invitation of the Pimicikamak government to learn what has happened in the community in the intervening years.

1.

The driver comes in the morning to pick me up and take me to meet Jackson Osborne, a local Elder and historian who has been documenting the effects of the dam on the lake. His name is Donald, a young man with a shaved head, round glasses, and a quiet air. We head back north along the lake in silence. We pass a skate park and come to a driveway that serves three houses. Several dogs roam the yard. It seems like everyone has dogs here, and no one keeps them inside.

Jackson's house is small and modest, an actually constructed house unlike the prefabricated trailers we saw in town. When Donald knocks, Jackson does not answer.

'Maybe he's not home?'

'No, he's home,' says Donald. I'm not sure how he knows; perhaps he knows Jackson's car, or perhaps there is nowhere for Jackson to go. Donald opens the door. It slides across a little square of cardboard that has been laid inside the house to collect the ubiquitous mud. Donald calls out Jackson's name across the small living room. Jackson comes around the corner from the kitchen area. He is a small man with inquisitive eyes blinking behind big glasses. He is wearing a blue housecoat and has a jar of instant coffee in one hand and a tablespoon in the other. It's obvious he is not expecting us.

Donald explains, 'Jackson, this is Kazim. He grew up in Jenpeg when they were building the dam. He's come back to find out what is happening in Cross Lake.'

Jackson's eyes light up and he nearly crows with excitement, 'You've come back! You came back to see us!' He gestures us in and guides me toward the table while he bustles around the kitchen making coffee for us.

The kettle is barely on the stove when he exclaims, 'I have so much to show you!' and before I can say anything in response, he is off, disappearing up a short flight of stairs off the living room, which must lead to the bedrooms. I hear him clapping his hands and talking to himself. Donald smiles a small smile. We hear much shuffling of papers and the sounds of drawers being opened and shut. Jackson reappears with two shoeboxes, which he places on the table between us, dragging his chair around so it's next to mine. He sits and opens the boxes. They are full of photographs.

'Look at these,' he says. 'These are photographs of Cross Lake. I go out in all different times of the year and take pictures of lakeshore so I can track the changes. See these shores?' He points to the shoreline in the photographs. He turns one photo over, and written there in spidery ballpoint is *Oct. 1989*. 'Later I'll take you out to the same place and show you the photograph and show you the shore, and you can see for yourself.'

We sit and drink coffee while he pulls more photographs out of boxes to show to Donald and me.

'How many pictures do you have?' I ask him.

'Oh, these are only part of them. I've been taking pictures going back to the 1980s. I didn't start out taking pictures though. I started out trying to get the schools to teach Cree language. My whole family was in the residential school system, you know.'

'I guess most of the older people in Cross Lake were,' I say.

'That's right. And the whole time my family was in there, we were serving Canada. My great-grandfather, James Whiskey, he fought for Canada and was killed in the First World War. And even though I have all these pictures here, we don't have any pictures of him and no medals, nothing to remember him by.'

He gets up to pour the coffee and brings the cups back to the table for the three of us. 'I have never even been to his burial place. It's in Europe somewhere, with the other Canadian soldiers.'

We're quiet for a moment, while we stir sugar into our cups.

'My sister went to the residential school and didn't come back,' he says then. 'Her name was Betsy. She caught tuberculosis in the school and was sent to Ninette, near Brandon, for medical testing. She died, but they never sent the body home. We don't even know where she is buried.'

I am silent. Jackson looks out the window. Donald doesn't say anything either. As I learn later, this kind of occurrence was not uncommon. Often the children who died in the residential schools, whether from the medical testing, from the rigours of hard labour, or from suicide, were buried in unmarked graves.

'Well, then in 2011, there was a monument built,' Jackson recounts, 'and a ceremony held for those who were subjected to medical testing, but my sister's name wasn't on the list of names.' He pauses. 'So now we don't know *what* happened to her, when she died or where. Or how.' In 2018, Anne Lindsay, a researcher in Brandon, was able to locate the grave of fifty children from the residential school, in what is now an RV park, by following a map that was hand-drawn for her by one of the residential school survivors. In contrast, there is still little information about the tuberculosis patients who were sent to the sanatorium in Ninette. One former employee claimed in 2009 that there were upwards of 200 former patients buried in underbrush a short drive from the facility.

Jackson's family, like mine, is connected to the dam: his father worked as a porter and guide for the original Manitoba Hydro team that surveyed the river in 1964. 'Oh, he was always happy, always cracking jokes. Here's some pictures of him with the team,' he says, passing them over. In all the pictures I see of Charlie Osborne, he is smiling. In one of them, Charlie is wearing the camp cook's white hat and apron and is pretending to cook.

'Later,' continues Jackson, 'after the survey was complete and Hydro built the dam and the water levels started fluctuating, he came to regret the work he did in helping the team to do the survey of the river. He is the one who told me to get a camera, to take pictures and document everything that was happening because of the dam.'

To this day, Jackson goes out regularly at all times of the day and in all seasons of the year to take photographs of the same views of the shoreline, so he can collate them together and assemble evidence of the shore erosion. He began in 1988, he tells me, around ten years after the dam opened.

'Do you have any photographs?' he asks suddenly. 'From before the dam was there? Do you think there are any early photographs in your parents' house? We don't have any here. All we have is the memory of the Elders.'

'I don't think so, Jackson. But I will check.' Even as I am saying this I am quite sure my parents don't have anything like that.

Suddenly Jackson reaches out and takes my hand and holds it in both of his. 'Thank God you came. You are the first person who came back.'

I'm a little surprised. 'No one else from Jenpeg has come here in the past forty years?'

'From Hydro, sure. From the government, sure. Other people come too. Robert Kennedy Jr. came. Someone from the United Nations came once. But no one from the town. No one who lived there. Not out here to Cross Lake. People from Jenpeg used to drive over and buy our crafts, buy gloves and moccasins and mukluks. But then they left and went back to cities. They never came back. You grew up here. You lived here. You're part of this land. This was your home, wasn't it? You're like us.'

He stops and lifts his hands up toward the ceiling dramatically. 'You've come back! Oh thank God for bringing you back!'

I smile at his passion even though I doubt I will be able to fulfill whatever hopes he is hanging on my presence.

'What would you do if others from Jenpeg came?' I want to know. 'I want to talk to them, the people who lived in Jenpeg and helped build the dam. They should know what happened.'

I promise that eventually I will share what I learn with everyone, with as many people as I can reach, anyhow. It occurs to me that not only the people who lived in Jenpeg but also any person who receives power from this dam ought to know what is happening.

We continue to look at his photographs. He shows me some big floating branches in the river. What happens, he explains, is that because of shore erosion, after the trunks rot and the soil breaks apart, the root systems of the dead trees float off into the river. They are called 'spiders' and they interfere with the motors of boats and sometimes cause them to capsize.

The water rises and falls because of the dam, the shore is chewed away, and the trees die; in the pictures Jackson shows me it almost looks like a tornado has come through and shattered those trees.

'People get trapped,' he says. 'Sometimes they drown.' He looks down at his hands.

He says, more softly, 'I wish your dad could come here.'

I say, 'I bet he would like it here. When you talk to me you can imagine that you are talking to him. I will tell him what you say.'

But I wonder how I will be able to explain all of this.

'It isn't only the people who live in Pimicikamak who have suffered,' says Jackson then. 'Even the animals who used to live with us don't come around Cross Lake anymore.'

Changes in silt levels have made Cross Lake's water undrinkable, and sediment has affected the spawning patterns of local fish populations: now the sturgeon, the whitefish, and the pickerel are gone. And without the fish, the muskrats, the wolverines, the bears, and the beavers are gone, too; there's no more trapping and there's very little hunting. One has to drive far out past the old traplines to hunt for deer and moose, Jackson says. Some people commission small planes to fly them even farther, often several hundred kilometres into the forest, to hunt.

There is another community, Norway House, which is at the main channel of the Nelson River where it comes into Lake Winnipeg, and where the sturgeons used to spawn. A team led by Annemieke Farenhorst in the Department of Soil Science at the University of Manitoba came here to study the drinking water and changes in the lake's ecosystem due to construction of the Jenpeg Generating Station. One of the researchers, Johanna Theroux, was able to show that silt levels had, in fact, increased due to Manitoba Hydro's dredging of two natural channels from the Nelson River into Lake Winnipeg. The work was done in the 1970s in order to intensify flow and maximize potential hydroelectric energy. Yet, the waters at Norway House seemed unaffected: most of the silt from resulting erosion was being carried into the western channel, bypassing Norway House and more heavily impacting the waters around the community of Cross Lake.

How was this allowed to happen? The province began surveying the northern river systems in the mid-1960s; by 1971 it had determined, based on a survey report, that the Nelson was ideal for generating hydroelectricity and that its flow could be increased by diverting several other rivers into the Nelson both before and after the dam. Brian Grover, the leader of the original survey team, wrote that the waters of the Nelson were 'clear, of high quality, so clean and fresh that we drank it directly from the river.'

The province set about negotiating the terms with the five First Nations that would be affected by the changes in water level. These included Cross Lake, Nelson House, Norway House, Split Lake, and York Factory, a community that had been previously relocated from their original site at the mouth of Nelson River on Hudson Bay. Although construction began in 1974, it wasn't until 1977 that the five bands came to terms with Manitoba Hydro, the provincial government, and the federal government in a treaty called the Northern Flood Agreement (NFA).

'Do you have a copy of the actual treaty?' I ask Jackson.

'I do!' he exclaims, jumping up and hurrying up the small staircase and down the corridor again. He emerges again with a sheaf of photocopied papers held together by an old-fashioned metal fastener like we used to use in school.

We sit and peruse the treaty. It's a slender document, running about seventy-five pages and full of legal language that traffics in promises to remediate the environmental impact of the dam, even while it is careful to say such outcomes are unknown and unpredictable and full remediation may prove impossible. The bulk of its pages are devoted to legal processes, describing terms and defining arbitration and implementation structures. The pages that make actual agreements with the bands are few and sparse in details, even though at the very beginning of the document all parties agree unequivocally, 'As a result of the Project, the water regime of certain waters, rivers, lakes, and streams has been or will be modified.' Somewhat more ominously, all parties also agree that it is 'not possible to foresee all adverse results' of the dam's construction. Accepting an offer to compensate each participating band with a 4:1 ratio of acres in exchange for lands ceded, the Cross Lake Band surrendered all land on their reserve contiguous to the Nelson River and lower than 690 feet above sea level.

An essential part of the treaty was a promise by Manitoba Hydro that they would 'control the flow of water on the regulated waterways so they do not exceed 687 feet above sea level' and that they would 'prevent inundation of Reserve lands.' Neither of these provisions has been effectively managed. It was in light of these abrogations that in 2014 the Pimicikamak contested Manitoba Hydro's rights to those ceded lands by occupying the site of the Jenpeg Generating Station and serving eviction papers.

Other parts of the treaty deal with ensuring potability of water from the lake, preservation of archeological and cultural sites, management of wildlife resources, and funding for social, economic, and cultural development in Cross Lake.

Most people I meet in Cross Lake know vaguely about the terms of the treaty but not the specifics. I can't really blame them. The treaty is not strong on specifics. I can only imagine that the chiefs who signed for the Cross Lake Band signed in good faith that the province and the federal government would follow through on their avowed intentions, and perhaps out of a realization that the dam – the construction of which had already begun, though treaty negotiations were still ongoing – was inevitable.

In the years after the construction of the dam, when the environmental impacts had become known and when the stated promises of the Northern Flood Agreement for support of economic and social development as well as environmental protections were abrogated, Brian Grover came to regret his role in surveying the river and enabling construction of the dam. The extreme underdevelopment in Cross Lake, the community that had participated in the surveys and had hosted and assisted with the building of the dam, distressed him.

'First Nations people,' he wrote in his 2016 memoir *The Summer of '64 on the Nelson River*, 'who were present long before immigrant settlers arrived from many other countries, should be able to enjoy the high standard of living which most other Canadians have achieved.' He recognized that the mineral and energy wealth of Indigenous peoples has been diverted and does not provide them with material benefits. Grover also speaks of Charlie Osborne's regret: 'Charlie [...] told his family that he regretted having done the work he did – with me and with many other technical people from southern communities. He stated that he would not have done this work if he had understood the consequences which followed.' His book is dedicated to the four members of his survey team from Cross Lake including Charlie Osborne.

As it happens, Grover's renewed interest and the writing of his memoir stemmed from the same sense of urgency that drew me back to Jenpeg and Cross Lake – the suicide epidemic in the winter of 2016. Grover had realized that while the vast majority of benefits from the dams in the North go to residents of the southern parts of the provinces – and also to some northern US cities in Minnesota and North Dakota – the environmental, economic, and social costs are borne by the northern Indigenous populations.

As Grover points out, because the difference in elevation between Lake Winnipeg and Hudson Bay is more than two hundred metres, the waterway that connects them is especially valuable as a source of hydroelectric power; besides the Jenpeg Generating Station, there are three other dams across the Nelson River on its way to Hudson Bay, and most of the smaller rivers and streams on the route have been diverted into the Nelson to increase its flow. These diversions along the waterways of the North have caused immense shore erosion, including here in Cross Lake. The disruption of normal water flow across the province has resulted in intermittent flooding for towns abutting the major lakes, even in the South, that disproportionately affect Indigenous communities.

Lake St. Martin is probably the most famous recent example: in 2011 there was a large and irregular spring runoff in the streams and rivers around the city of Winnipeg; to protect valuable properties there, the province diverted floodwaters onto reserve land. The community of Lake St. Martin was evacuated and subsequently destroyed by the floodwaters. For six years the lost town's nearly 1,5000 residents lived in temporary housing in Winnipeg. Only in 2017 were some of the residents finally resettled back in Lake St. Martin; ninety-two elderly members of the community had died in the intervening years. As of early 2020, approximately 314 families were still waiting for housing to be built so they could return home. Those who had already returned were still lacking jobs, healthcare facilities, and social services.

Jackson recounted to me other ways the relationship with the lake has changed. Aside from the so-called 'spiders,' the massive broken tree roots that float away and get caught in the propellers of motorboats, some of the small islands where people used to live have been flooded and made uninhabitable; all of their residents had to be evacuated to the mainland.

'The lake is an essential part of our identity here,' says Jackson. 'The water is as sacred to us as the land.'

Cree lands all across northern Canada were connected not only by the free-flowing water but by culture and language. The Pimicikamak way of life was sustainable, from the abundance of fishing, hunting, and trapping, supplemented by the relatively fertile agriculture of the water-fed region. So tied to their livelihood is their connection to water that the people of Pimicikamak once called themselves *nickikonakos* – 'otter people.'

'We are not just trying to save the lake and the fish, but we are trying to save ourselves as a people,' Jackson insists.

He takes us back into the room where he has stored his archives. It's small, and seems to still be serving as someone's bedroom, probably a child's. There's a single bed propped up on top of two dressers on one side, and a desk and filing cabinets on the other side. He pulls another big box out from under the desk. 'I have some videos in here, too.'

On the corkboard above the desk there is a beautiful ink drawing of an abstract design, sort of like clouds. 'Who did this?' I ask, touching the drawing.

'Oh, my nephew Charlton. He was an artist. I have a folder with his drawings.' He pulls out a folder bulging with scraps of paper and drawings – of people, of animals, wild abstractions.

'Where is he now?' I ask, afraid of the answer.

'He drowned on the lake,' says Jackson. 'His boat was capsized by a spider and they didn't get out there in time to save him.'

I don't say anything.

'Come on,' he says. 'Let's take a drive.'

2.

We drive out, Donald and Jackson and I, to see the places where the water has flooded the lands, where the shore has eroded away.

On our drive, I am captivated anew by the quality of the northern light. It always looks like it's been raining: the yellow-white golden colour of the dry grasses; the muted green of fir trees and the wet black of their trunks, with pale, dirty-white paper birches interspersed; blue smoke of the clouds, and then luminous and dark grey, the soft, heavy sky billows pulsing with incipient light above. The lake – broken branches rising here and there above the water – seems resentful, treacherous, resigned.

By the side of the road there is an overturned car, which, judging by its condition, has been lying there for some time. I see more prefab houses, and a swing set in the small backyard of a scrubby lawn: this could have been ours, in Jenpeg. I am reminded so much of that town, so close to here.

At Jackson's direction, Donald pulls over and we clamber out of the car. 'Okay, now close your eyes,' Jackson instructs, then guides me across the road to its shoulder, facing the lake. 'Now open your eyes.'

Jackson is holding up a photograph in front of my face. I can see the actual lake to the left and right, and he is holding the picture so I can see the continuous shoreline and a small sandy beach with a promontory of three large boulders. 'This picture is from ten years ago,' he says.

'Now look.' And his arm drops away so I can see the shore now.

'The whole beach is gone!' I exclaim. 'Those protruding rocks, too.'

'They're all underwater,' Jackson says, pointing in the direction where the rocks lie submerged.

We continue down the road in the same direction and come to a house on the lake. Jackson shows me a photograph of the house from some fifteen years ago: the backyard abuts a small bluff with a sandy beach below. When I look up from the photograph, I see that half the yard has been eroded away into muck and weeds by the rising and falling lake.

In other places, especially along the roadway, they have put in stony riprap to try to restrain the erosion, but this hasn't appeared to work. While the flooding at Lake St. Martin was the result of the province diverting water during a larger-than-expected seasonal over-flow, flooding in Indigenous communities because of dams is all too common. British Columbia's W. A. C. Bennett Dam, constructed in 1968, flooded out five First Nations communities, which were all forced to relocate. Although BC Hydro settled multi-million dollar suits with the communities, this was largely seen as a compromise in order to gain support for a new proposed dam on the same river.

Jackson takes me to other places along the lake, and he holds up more pictures of the same view – from twenty years ago, then ten years ago – to compare with today. I can see with my own eyes how the water is pulling the shore apart. The lake's water level always pulsed, but it pulsed with natural seasonal rhythms. Now, as documented by Farenhorst and her team in the research conducted at Norway House and elsewhere along the Nelson River watershed, the more dramatic fluctuations resulting from damming have caused this widespread shoreline erosion.

In addition, logging companies in the region are clear-cutting timber to be made into lumber and sold, Jackson says. 'Trees are oxygen-giving, they are medicine to the people, and they are our property and our resource. They should not be taken away from us.'

At the same time, the Pimicikamak can't engage in their own forestry operations, because the timber, and access to it, are controlled by federal Canadian laws. Jackson says, 'If the beaver doesn't need permission to cut a tree, then neither should we.'

The calm surface of the water belies the damage that occurs because of the disturbed tree roots and rocks. The debris must be cleared constantly or it floats out into the lake in the form of those dangerous spiders Jackson showed me pictures of; not only can they capsize smaller boats, but they are hazardous to larger boats, as they can break their propellers and damage their hulls.

During construction of the Jenpeg Generating Station, Manitoba premier Ed Schreyer promised that water levels would not change beyond the negotiated limits, and this provision was written into the Northern Flood Agreement. During a 1975 press conference announcing the plan, he famously held up a pencil to reporters and vowed that the water level would only fluctuate the length of that pencil. Forty years later, in response to the 2014 occupation of the Jenpeg Generating Station and the Pimicikamak council serving eviction papers to the province and Manitoba Hydro, Premier Greg Selinger – whose deputy premier was Eric Robinson, an Asiniskawiyiniwak Cree from Norway House and a survivor of the residential school system–issued a formal apology for the economic and social damage from hydroelectric development, acknowledging that the province had vastly underestimated the impact of the dam. Jackson Osborne commented to the CBC, 'The premier should apologize to the muskrats, to the beavers, to the fish, to the moose.' For his part, Schreyer – who went on to become Governor General of Canada – came to oppose future-planned Manitoba Hydro projects as too expensive, and was supportive of wind and solar energy as cheaper alternatives to additional hydroelectric development.

What a rush of feeling had come over me when we first drove across the causeway from the airport – the golden reeds and dark brown bulrushes transporting me back in time. I stand now at the cold shore, looking out at the deep-blue lake, the washed-out sky, the bright yellow grasses. 'It's so beautiful,' I say.

Jackson hears me and cries out, 'No! Don't say that!'

I turn around, surprised.

'I don't like it when people say that Cross Lake is beautiful. Because I remember what it was like before. You think you see beauty but you are looking at ruins, ruins of the land and the water.'

'But it's so much like what I remember from my childhood.'

'It isn't,' he says sadly, holding out the photographs he had been showing. 'You have *seen* that it isn't.'

'How did they not know this was going to happen?' I say to no one in particular.

'It was just government people who came, and geologists and surveyors and engineers,' says Jackson. 'There were no professors, no biologists who were thinking about the animals and the trees.'

He's right. Those who built the dam were thinking about what the river could produce, not about the whole community of plants and animals that it was the centre of. They were thinking about power: water flow and wattage. How could I have thought this place was like a home to me? My mother was right: we lived here for only a few years. I had no claim to it. What is the connection between a person and the land he lives on? Then again, what government or document can legislate that stirring of belongingness born in the heart?

The lake is as much a part of daily life in Pimicikamak as it was before, but now the water has become erratic – the fluctuations are extreme, the countermeasures half-hearted – and people are disconnected from the water's bounties. The lake is an adversary now, something to contend with, and most of the fish and muskrats and beaver are gone, game animals drifting farther away, the food chain compromised. The lake itself is unsafe and the relationships between people and environment, joined for so many countless thousands of years, are now severed.

Between 1992 and 1997, the four other signatories to the Northern Flood Agreement – Asiniskawiyiniwak (Norway House), which is upriver from Cross Lake and the Pimicikamak lands, along with Nisichawayasihk (Nelson House), Kihciwaskahihan (York Factory), and Tataskweyak (Split Lake), all farther downriver, closer to Hudson Bay – renegotiated their terms with Manitoba Hydro in detailed implementation agreements that range from 200 to 500 pages. The Pimicikamak of Cross Lake alone refused to concede terms in a revised implementation agreement, though the community of Pimicikamak Cree that lives across the reserve border on federal and provincial land came to their own separate agreement with Manitoba Hydro in 2010, including an approximately $9 million settlement and a promise of subsidized electricity. And, as part of that new agreement, they incorporated as a provincial town with the same name, Cross Lake. There are some tensions between the communities; for instance, while the reserve is dry, and committedly so, there is a liquor store in the provincial town of Cross Lake, right across the border from the reserve community of Cross Lake.

It's getting colder – five degrees Celsius – and darker, so we drive on to the motel. Jackson jokes with me on the ride home: 'You Americans want to chide your president because he did not win the popular vote, while we in Pimicikamak tell the Canadian politicians, "You never won the *poplar* vote!"'

Jackson is laughing at his pun, but the joke points to a deeper truth about how 'territory' is viewed culturally; rather than as topography (for military conquest or property-surveying purposes) or as geology (to delineate mineral wealth and resources), the Cree view of the landscape includes people, animals, trees, other plant life, the water itself, and even the rocks and soil and dirt as equal components. Why shouldn't the poplar trees have a vote?

Tomorrow, I am planning to travel out to see the Jenpeg Generating Station and then drive on to the town site, which lies somewhat beyond and, as far as I know, may have been reclaimed by the forest. I am not sure where to find the old town, so I log in to an online group composed of former Hydro employees who were Jenpeg residents and ask whether anyone knows the exact coordinates. One of the men writes back and says that as recently as the late 1990s the streets were still there, though grown over. He explains something about the plumbing infrastructure underground keeping at least the outline of the streets visible, so I don't worry too much about finding something, as long as someone at the dam can point us in the right direction.

So what happens when I go back to Jenpeg? What if I go back and find some trace, whether physical or internal, of the town I've always dreamed of? What then? We left – me, my family, all the people who lived here. We left and we never looked back, only went on flipping switches off and on in our houses, our fingers on the plastic, never feeling that rush of current through the wires, the rush of water through the land.

HOW TO SMALL
Oana Avasilichioaei and Erín Moure

How to language. How its wealth.

                              wind tremors above
How to find language in life's commonplaces and have it mean.

              water
How to live in language that opens language to language, opens us to
one another, language that humanes us.

                              grasses, bitter grass
How to water. How to auga. How to eau. How to apa.

                              rain cups light in leaves
How to fear and grow.

How to open hands justly.

How to think into foreign. How to not stop, not obstacle, not fear
the foreign.

                              wind-quake at water's arrival
How to small the small the small.

How to not monopolize, monospeak, monouse, monothink, monobe.

                              frost silting a stream
How to hands.

              sea-bitter herbs
How to hands open. How to give over to words imperatively.

How to cultivate palms in language soils. How to seed words and
each other anew.

How to translate the hands to the throat. How to translate the throat
to the hands.

                              până când cineva

How to throat.

if, then

How to soil the soil with soil. see yet

the grasses?

How to be water.

How to unmanifest the manifest.

crests waves to

How to signature the 'I.' How to lose its singularity and become a flock of sparrows suddened by a wind.   'smudge' 'pluck'

How to unnature our natures.

How to question. How to be questioned. How to question again. How to be questioned again.

We could not shatter better, yet

How to threshold the threshold. How to live in the crossings of a threshold.

How to unborder a border. How to unmean, unwar, unnormalize a border.

How to unborder a language's borders.

Poţi   construi   un   mic   oraş

How to material a word's meat. How to cuvânt un vânt.

J'évoquerai le livre et
provoquerai les questions. – Edmond Jabès

How to read a leaf's technology. How to green the green of green's arteries.

let a linden flower

In the small of throat's heat, its soft word, how to breathe.

'r' = 'v'

The pacing? Pronoun who? 'The Latin conscience is complicit. Messenger. Fantasy. Derision. Ache and symptom. What can be healed out of this adversity?' The crushed light of the ear, clearly hears.

[folds in roadways]

[folds in skylights]

[folds in tingling]

SUDBURY
Jonathan Ball

In the dream
He opens his hands
To see what he has caught
And in that instant
It escapes

It is gone so fast
It is only a blur
Sometimes
That is the way
True things are

In the dream
She is shivering
But she does not know
Why, and when she wakes
She is cold, so cold

It is the middle
Of the summer
And her lover lies
Awake, uncomfortable
In the heat

In the dream
The child sees rivers
Still and clear
Like the lake where the poison
From the neighbouring factories

Has killed everything
In the water and now
Huge boulders at the bottom
Of its terrible depths
Appear as pebbles in shallow water

The child tries
To grab a pretty stone
But falls in, drowning
As the liquid burns
His lungs and eyes

ANEMONE
Erin Robinsong

Eye of the sea

portals, orifices

mouths that see

turquoise anus flowering

cosmic vaginas

give birth through the mouth

of the sea.

This is the situation –
This is the situation –

Esther says it's not that the climate depends on what we do or don't do –
it's that we depend entirely on climate

to travel into reality with
to think

with anemones, lavishly
and without money

through cracks in existence
named Bezos Gates Buffett Arnault Ortego Slim Zuckerberg Walton
Koch Bloomberg

who offer such drab death
to everyone.

Will you buy this water, this air, this chemo
Will you accept man-made apocalypse with no men to answer
                                          to cosmic generosity –

or pleasure from the sun
while pleasuring the moon?

ON RADIANCE
Adrian De Leon

All of the luminaries, all of that desperate brilliance.
– David Chariandy, 'As Man'

Once, I dreamed that two suns rose over Scarborough. One glided in the usual way, from east to west, the stuff of aubades and nocturnes of epochs past. The other mushroomed from its concrete ruins below. Whereas that first sun gifted us with life and quotidian rhythm, the second sank us into a painful night. Its rays of atomic cloud roared across the subdivisions and tore their way through the plazas, incessantly radiating to annihilation. Amidst those nightmare tosses, I scornfully gave that second sun a name: Pickering.

From my Southeast Scarborough bedroom, the Pickering Nuclear Generating Station never let me forget its presence. My neighbourhood was quiet, save for the sharp bouncing of Spalding against concrete. Every night, the breeze outside hummed with the dissonant chord of the GO train, south of Pixley Crescent. But some afternoons, a poltergeist bellowed in the sky from the east. The power plant's low *whoop whoop* haunted my slice of West Hill with an oppressive weight long after the sirens ceased. Even if they signalled some safety test or routine maintenance, the power plant's call always reminded me of imminent destruction.

Completed in 1986, the Pickering Nuclear Generating Station promised thirty years of a bright Ontario. Once the shining star of Canadian technology, it has since pumped more toxic waste than usable energy into the shoreline. For decades, the Nuclear Waste Management Organization has been looking for a 'willing host' for all the toxic waste kept under the edifice. Meanwhile, we, the unwilling hosts, incubated the 36,000-ton monster below. As teenagers, we imagined radiation creeping through the subterranean like tendrils ready to snatch at our ankles.

We felt the slow death percolate beneath the pristine soles of our Air Force 1s. *Memento mori.*

↓

In high school history classes, the power plant to the east took on new meaning. Mr. Silver made his way through the bloody campaigns in Europe. He took extra care to mention where Canadian troops made their contributions to the war effort. Suddenly, a bomb dropped on Pearl Harbor, and two minutes into the lecture later, two bigger bombs dropped on Japan. Perhaps some sideshow 'skirmishes' in the Philippines, or along China's port cities, places that some of us in the classroom called our estranged homes. Then, to end the war, that nightmare sun mushrooming over Hiroshima, which they called Little Boy. His obese brother, Fat Man, somersaulted upon Nagasaki, remembered but hardly as commemorated as Hiroshima. An after-thought, like Scarborough. In the linoleum blackness of our class-rooms, we felt like little Nagasakis.

Brenton, my token white friend in graduate school, often lectures me over sour beers about Nagasaki. I listen to him mid-pucker as he constellates across the history of the nuclear world. Hiroshima, the brightest one. At war's 'end.' Nagasaki, the other bomb. No fanfares, except after Hiroshima. Then, like the Greek storytellers of old, Brenton connects other dots in the historical backdrop. Great Bear Lake brightens into focus, illuminating Dene workers' helmets in plutonium mines. He traces a finger down to New Mexico, the nuclear age's testing grounds, craters of Diné homes. Westward, in the deep blue of my inaugural ocean, the Bikini Atoll and the many bombshells since.

Soon enough, other stars, those celestial explosions, expanded upon the terrible tales etched in the sky. Professional warmonger Dwight Eisenhower declared that his harbingers of death could be used for peace. If we could contain more Fat Men in insulated concrete tombs, these bombs would be peaceful. All over the world, Atoms for Peace produced little Nagasakis, dying stars churning at the brink of nuclear disaster, offering the radiant promise of employment and boundless energy. Chernobyl, that Soviet Nagasaki, could not cradle its detonations from its fleeing denizens. And Fukushima, the most recent supernova, carried its detritus eastward along the maelstroms that slowly sink the sea of islands.

If I squint hard enough, the stars make the shape of the Pickering power plant.

♦

Amidst these atomic fever dreams, new celestial forms congealed in the chaotic galaxy called Scarborough. The radiation stirred below from the deaths of tiny stars that powered our homes. Above, explosions from the hatred of mediocre white men on bully pulpits. Steely glares from police flashlights underneath the Gardiner and along Orton Park. News cameras amidst the maroon of Hennessy and scarlet of sidewalks. In between, some of us pulled together in the immense gravity from which we speculated constellations yet to come. We forged commons amidst the little nebulae of our neighbourhoods.

Along the crests of the Rouge Valley, our creative writing classrooms flourished in that gravity. In front of the light of a PowerPoint projection, Daniel absorbed the brilliance from his students. Natasha flashed with fictions sparking from the embers of hip-hop bass in her chest. I wrote under the flicker of subway lights and the glint of a loaded gun. With her pen, Oubah made the pink of gums glow like the Pleiades. Like their own Hubble Space Telescopes, Chelsea and Leanne pulled light-years from the darkness into their fictions. And Téa, our East-End prophet, recited new zodiacs from the star clusters of Galloway windows.

Fittingly, we found our stories beneath the grimy skylights of the Meeting Place. This edifice lies adjacent to the maze of the Humanities Wing, Brutalist fortress walls in the bosom of the Rouge Valley's embrace. These darlings of the architect John Andrews traced stairways to heaven. Each step a grey prism reaching for the clouds, relics of an era when formless sludge congealed into modernist Babels, the poetry of hard labour.

Eastward, other prisms of concrete in the sky: the Pickering power plant.

⚘

While the plant's grey shapes interrupt the azure pool up above, other roots and grasses caress the waters flowing into the cerulean of the Leading Sea. A mighty river named Red inaugurates in two places. The western mouth speaks its gospel underneath the Orton Park bridge. The eastern lips smile into the reeds, in the company of families casting their rods into the deep.

At the edge of this eastern mouth, sand blankets the shores, and oceanic breezes billow against the low trees. Melanin-rich gatherings unwrap nostalgia for their tropic homes across the sand, culinary homelands in their Tupperwares laid across the fabric. Underneath the rusty bridge, a verdant train periodically interrupts newcomers' first forays into Rouge Beach Park. Three trains later, and the horns join the blaring bass of reggaeton, the folding waves against our feet, the cheers and jeers from the badminton game. Just another rhythm of Scarborough life.

Walking west along the tracks, the brush obscures the paper-thin blue horizon. We salvage branches for the firepit and toss half-baked Backwoods into the stack. Justin wraps shallots and enoki bunches in aluminum foil, and scatters them in the heated sand. Katie commandeers the troops through the trees to gather firewood in her Schomburg wilderness way. Jason and Mauriene playfully Super Mario down the boulders to gather at their alcoves. Pat steals away with the cafe girl and two waffle cones. Fateha makes believe a Bay of Bengal with every shoreline splash. Several yards away, smoky shadows of other Scarborough kids who dare to dance so close to destruction.

On the shores of the Leading Sea, Scarborough sets with many suns. The first casts its dying embers across the horizon, tempered by the coal silhouettes of the Bluffs. The other bonfire suns dot the secret clearings of makeshift beaches.

Radiant little lives in the tow of a dying star.

Three academic works inform this essay: Teresia K. Teaiwa, 'bikinis and other s/pacific n/oceans' (1994); Lisa Yoneyama, *Hiroshima Traces: Time, Space, and the Dialectics of Memory* (1999); and Peter C. Van Wyck, *The Highway of the Atom* (2010). The author thanks the good folks of Scarborough and adjacents in the making of this essay.

AMATEUR KITTENS DREAMING SOLAR ENERGY
Jacob Wren

If humanity survives, which is unlikely, people will want to know what it was like. This feeling that the end was no longer happening in some distant future but was basically happening now. The conversations quoting scientists who had warned us before it was too late but had not known how to summon enough political will for enough people to act, for a large enough number of people to heed their far-too-prescient warnings. The conversations in which we tried to reassure each other in the knowledge that despair or hopelessness would solve nothing and were in fact the emotions – understandable as they might be – that were the exact opposite of what was required. They will want to know what it was like, search for insights as to why we didn't do more to save them, to save ourselves. We will want to know what it was like.

I am sitting here staring out the window on a calm Monday evening. At the moment it is like nothing. It is like every other unmemorable Monday evening I am able to recall. This week has been unseasonably cool, a relief, a break from the heat of the previous weeks. I am living without internet at home because I am too addicted to the internet and, if I had it, I would be staring at it now, completely mesmerized by the screen, instead of writing these words. I of course wonder if there's any point in writing these words. Historically, literature was built by writers who each had at least some feeling there was a chance their writing might live on, that someone might continue to read them far into the future. Statistically the odds for this were not good, and therefore literature has also been built, layer by layer, upon misguided fantasies of posterity. But sitting here with no internet, staring mindlessly out the window, it is extremely difficult for me to imagine any distant future in which someone might be reading these words. Yet imagine it I do. Because I'm a writer and therefore can't help myself. And when I imagine it, I also can't help but feel their hunger, their longing to know just what it is like

– right here, right now – and I search desperately, both within myself and directly out the window at the quiet street in front of me, searching for something to tell them.

If I were online I would see that the glaciers in Iceland are melting and the forests in the Amazon are burning. I already know the glaciers are melting and the forests are burning. I know and everyone I know also knows. Such knowledge requires action but the actions immediately available to us don't feel especially clear. Those fighting for the continued use of oil and plastic have considerably more power and resources than all of us protesting against them. But, of course, giving up would be equally insane.

Later tonight I have a date. I have not been out on a date in a very long time. I don't know what compelled me to say yes. Someone, not even a friend, more of an acquaintance, set us up. I don't actually remember if that's ever happened in my life before: someone I know suggesting I meet someone I don't know for a drink. I don't think I've ever tried to play matchmaker. If I imagine people I know, who are single or semi-single or polyamorous, I don't find myself imagining any of them hooking up with each other, in any of the various combinations, or for that matter getting together with anyone else. I wonder why I don't imagine such things. For a moment I suspect that maybe there's something similar in my inability to imagine acquaintances or friends in bed together and my inability to imagine the distant future. Maybe there's nothing so consequent about this analogy since really all they have in common is a certain lack of imagination on my part. And yet these days the world needs all the imagination it can get.

HOW TO SURVIVE IN A TIME OF GREAT URGENCY

Jody Chan

> *after Solmaz Sharif*

to fill the prescription

to arrange a rotten avocado on toast

to misplace the keys

to don shorts as the fires stretch, second by unimaginable second,
  into September

to imagine yourself choking on chemical sky

to dismount at the wrong streetcar stop, three nights in a row

to locate fear in the sternum, smoke-skinned, ashy-lipped

to recall that Audre Lorde once named her anger *a boiling hot spring
  likely to erupt at any point, leaping out of my consciousness like a
  fire on the landscape*

to consider the crisis being legislated into an infant committee, their
  urgent mandate

to attend your first political rally, then to rage at the bricked facade
  of the bureaucrat's office, every face around you unnamed

to fill your therapy hour with the delight of political discovery, with
  nicknames for your new awareness

to invoke June Jordan from a smartphone speaker, saying, *I can't do
  what I want to do with my own body because I am the wrong* –

to declare you are finished saying it nicely

to waggle your head over the headlines, unsurprised

to facilitate the meeting, wielding a stiff-armed, sharp-handed clock
  over each agenda item

to extol the well-worded email as a potent weapon of resistance,
  urgent every subject line

to deploy the word *opportunity* instead of the word *crisis* whenever
  possible

to learn to dislike every cop, to suspect everyone you dislike of being
  a cop

to not have somewhere to threaten relocation to, the way an American
   lover once said, *if things get worse I'm moving to Canada*
to declare homelessness no crisis and meanwhile the deaths amass
   by garbage truck, by clothing bin, by head-waggle
to go back to an empty house, to scroll countless Facebook statuses
   capitalizing on this state-sanctioned opportunity for critique
to hear the therapist ask, *where do you feel safety in your body*, to face
   her silently until the hour passes, not a single eyelash or toenail
   responding
to institute check-ins at every meeting, to never check in honestly
to mail a letter with no return address
to declare all of this not a crisis but a continuation
to wake up on the 9,262nd day of your life, the 9,255th without your
   mother, and realize you still miss her
to text your aunt and fumble the Cantonese for *protest*, for *police*
   budget, to try to consider this an opportunity for communication
to read her reply, *dog emoji* and *have you eaten yet?*
to sob in the bathroom at the elections viewing party, to hear the
   alarmed stranger in the next stall ask, *what's wrong*, and have no
   lines to say
to know the smell of crusted toothpaste, mould festooning the sink
to learn the tricks; that is, to visualize blenders, to identify colours,
   to palm a heavy stone
to wonder with June *who the hell set things up like this*
to attend your five-hundredth rally, the office, the faces the same,
   flanked by neon-vested police
to flick the blender on and off and on and off and on and on
to allow yourself *I don't know how to fix it*
to grieve someone 9,255 mornings and not be done with it
to locate sadness in the marble hallway of your throat, to attend, to
   wait on, to take care of it
to summon June Jordan from a smartphone speaker, how she said,
   from now on my resistance
my simple and daily and nightly self-determination

to picture at this moment Audre Lorde spreading a perfectly ripened
    avocado on toast
to revere the miracle of meeting snacks
to attend the party, while Prince and Whitney whistle urgent through
    your friends, their wine-beaded lips
to dance, then, to spin dizzy-footed revolutions, to wake your paining,
    hibernating hips
to refill the prescriptions
to stockpile inhalers
to allow an entire future this way, day by unimaginable day,
to arrive

CLIMATE ANXIETY
Trynne Delaney

the grocery store is out of tofu
in calgary.
o town that runs on beef and crude oil,
understocked soy blocks a sign of hope
when the city's usually just coughing
its way out of smoke this time of year.
now, instead,
the amazon's burning for profit
and everyone's so scared of death
they forget some of us will survive
The End –
mass extinction doesn't happen in a day!
yap the dinosaur jaws compressing below us
and if climate change is getting you down
you can send a gif of jeff goldblum
through a server system
that will burn as much fuel
as the airline industry
by 2020.
it's all pretty bleak
but you know, uh,
life, uh, finds a way.

ALL THIS TO SAY
Natalie Lim

when you want something badly enough,
it turns your stomach to coiled muscle.

when my hunger clenches this desperately
I am surprised blood does not pour

from my eyes, surprised always at how my body
protects me from the animal of itself.

I cried in the bathtub, on the bus,
in the Starbucks on Granville while strangers stared

but said nothing; I am the stranger
who stares and frowns, sips my latte in silence.

I place Amazon orders, buy spinach in bulk,
bring a reusable mug to save ten cents on coffee.

I forget my reusable mug,
write poetry while taking out the garbage.

an ocean away, the earth continues her burning
and I feel her clenching in on us,

protecting herself from these animals she carries,
our need for green numbers, upward arrows.

this brave new world, polished too bright.

all this to say that in the end, the last of us will run like blood
into her oceans, that maybe we deserved it,

that if we were kinder we might be worth
saving. I don't believe these words

but feel them in my gut like instinct, like an animal,
like a tide slowly rising

until it finally – blessedly –
sweeps me away.

ASHEN FIELDS
Ira Reinhart-Smith

Ashen fields

Their purpose yet to be revealed

Like blood congealed

Lies are spoken

Apologies now forsaken

Empty words for the empty field

Lies revealed

Fights on streets for the right of life

To them is it not trivial?

All of this?

Money is their blood all they know.

To live to die to lie for it is all they know.

It is all they know.

Ashen fields.

To them it is profits revealed.

The forest they say was 'profits concealed'

The frog would not have chosen the field.

REQUIES

Christiane Vadnais, translated from the French by Pablo Strauss

Fat translucent raindrops agglutinate like insect eggs on the glass, blurring the view. The eight men and women around the table are hopped up like a gang of teenagers. Some mock each other mercilessly, some scarf down this meal as if it were their last supper, drenching each mouthful in butter and cream, and others stare down at their plates with a palpable angst. Knife in hand, Alex gazes silently into the distance. The few who aren't hollering or stuffing their faces are staring out the window into a damp landscape that reminds them of the phlegmatic consistency of their own bodies beneath only a thin layer of skin.

They have long known they are protected by the armies of bacteria that colonize the pits of their stomachs. There was a time when yogourt commercials still made them laugh or, at worst, mildly uncomfortable. *Did you know there are more bacteria in the human intestine than there are people in the world!* Most had little trouble sweeping such information under the spotless rugs in their Scandinavian minimalist decors. Today, the thought of their inhabited stomachs, like the knowledge that the universe is expanding, triggers a nausea no pill can relieve. Just as it is hard to picture life developing light years away from their planet, the concept of matter becoming discontinuous on the cellular and atomic scales sickens them.

Like a ravenous sailor, Alex holds her knife perpendicular to the table, mainly to stop herself from turning it upside down, pointing the tip toward her skin, and plunging it into her body. The eight people gathered in this room are hyperaware of their bodies. Sometimes they spend pinched-lipped hours massaging their stomachs and staring out at the river as it overflows its bed. At other times they put every ounce of energy they have into reconciling their constituent parts. Then they slide into other people's beds and let out sighs, gentle exhalations warm and sweet as summer winds. Usually they can sense an energy, like the electrical charge that comes before a storm; it makes them want to run, and fight, scream at the seeping green sky and the filthy floodwaters. They are growing more agitated by the day.

There isn't much time left. When he notices Alex's posture, Lawrence leans against her shoulder, gently forcing the young woman to set the blade down on the tablecloth. He whispers something to her that the others can't hear, gives her hand a gentle squeeze, then gets back up again. He wants this touch to infuse her being, all the way to her heart. He wishes he could take her in his arms, take every one of them in his arms, make them forget the implacability of time and the permeability of their bodies. He wishes he could, with a single movement, normalize their breathing and blood flow and all the thoughts that haunt them.

In this frenzy, Alex's anxiety has gone unnoticed. To resist the urge to pick up the knife again, she sits with legs crossed and hands clasped, like a schoolgirl. She opens her mouth, as if some sound were waiting to come out, but soon shuts it. Then, without a word, she lunges forward. Her hands have ceased obeying her mind. Social niceties have fallen by the wayside. She spews up her meal all over her dress, with its gentle scent of laundry soap.

The room falls silent. Lawrence takes hold of Alex's arm and carefully sponges her clothes clean. Then nurse and dying patient get up together.

In the preceding days, the floodwaters had been closing in on their cabin like a trap. Even when the rains were at their most violent, the sick ones kept going outside – to run, to dance, to lie open-mouthed on the wet earth. They were no different then than they are now: furiously alive, exhausted, euphoric, convinced of their own ignorance and their ability to subsist at once in extreme excitement and the most profound fatigue, of their power to explode and to dissolve, like walking corpses or ecosystems on the verge of implosion. They had followed him of their own volition to this remote outpost – to mitigate the risk of contagion, escape the hysteria gripping the city, live out the last days before their extinction. The choice hadn't seemed irrevocable. Then they found themselves on an island, surrounded by water, stripped of any possibility of leaving. They're never going back.

Insects swarmed all around, but the animals they should have seen in these parts had been swept away by the floods. Only the birds remained, on perches high above the ground. From time to time they formed terrifying flocks and took flight, whirling around in the sky before diving back to earth. At the sight of this, some were visited by auguries of obscure purport and then left wondering whether they themselves – parasite-ridden earthbound mammals – might be prophets of doom. They asked question after question until they could no longer say for certain where their own beings ended or what lay beyond. Is it true that we are what we eat? Or are we rather what we breathe? The excreta and carbon dioxide and kinetic energy we pump back into nature? Were we really no more than the sum of our parts? Were we the clouds, the trees, the stones? If even microbiota were distinct from our organism, on a small enough scale, how could anyone say for sure where their own being stopped and the birds began?

Lawrence had never once lied to them. He cared for them, one and all; while they ran and screamed and cried and self-mutilated, he washed their clothes and cooked their meals. He gave them pills to ease their symptoms, made sure their rooms contained all they needed to rest in comfort. At the end of the day, they would fall into his arms and thank him for not forsaking them, for not building a raft to float away on. No one knew what lay behind his devotion, but all felt increasing gratitude. Some even found an unlikely levity. They would joke around before turning in for the night, let themselves gently drift toward the beds where they could close their eyes at last.

Some might claim Alex left them after hours of acute suffering. In truth it was over in a microsecond, like the flip of a circuit breaker.

She was there; then she wasn't. That woman who just yesterday had wielded her knife with a survivor's ferocity was now a lead-coloured lump at their feet. The world around them teems with life. In the river, in the puddles, under rocks, in every atom of the waterlogged earth in which they are digging a hole to lay their companion to rest. Worms, beetles, fungi, algae, viruses, protozoa. *Calliphora vicina.* Everything is inhabited: the sky and the forest, the river and the living soil whose every crevice overflows with water. Alex will not be buried alone; she will be laid in the ground with the agents of her own decomposition. They think about the foreign bodies living in her abdomen, the ones that constituted her for the length of the epidemic, and the period of quarantine out here in nature – long enough for the symptoms to mature, long enough for an ending. It's best not to read too much into it, they think, since the idea of her decomposing with these monsters enrages them. When they contemplate her, it's their own fate they see. They wish there was a way to rip open her stomach and yank out the interlopers, sew her lustreless skin together again, and slip one of her dresses onto her body. They hope against hope that in death we all become our one true, univocal self, but they know too well the opposite is true. Underground we just disintegrate. Each atom that made us who we were turns into something else – everyone imagines a tree or a plant or a flower. We'll just as likely return as a larva, or something equally repugnant and insignificant: a fungus.

In the group of men and women digging the hole, Lawrence stands out for his serene expression and smooth skull tilted toward the ground. But what truly sets him apart is his outfit and waterproof boots. Lawrence alone does not see his own future in Alex's fate; he alone is not bent double in pain. It is more a happy accident of good health than choice of profession that drives him to provide food and succour, to prop up cushions under their bedridden backs and place capsules on their tongues. When the river began its rise, no one worried about their supplies or how to get help. They already knew how the story would end. So they dig. They lay Alex's body in the hole and stare at her. The wind rises and falls without rhyme or reason, and the sky changes colour behind the clouds, shadows playing over the face of the person they came here to bury.

Though the corpse's cells have already begun to shrivel up and microscopic bacteria have set to work, the dead woman's features are so rigid that the group immediately notices the tiny opening between two pale, almost blue lips. They all see the hooklike thing slowly emerge from her mouth. It's the curved foot of a parasite. Petrified, they wait. Standing around the grave in a circle, they watch in horror as the creature's phosphorescent shell emerges from her body, then comes to rest in the dead centre of Alex's face.

The seven who remain exchange stupefied glances. Instantly and without discussion, they are of one mind: the thing that came out of the dead girl after her extinction is no longer part of her. As one, they throw themselves upon this creature, a swarm of enraged, vengeful hands rushing to fling it to the ground, where they crush and trample it until nothing remains but a small purée of cells and fluids.

Over the following days, the most unsettling memory will be not Alex's demise but the emergence of the parasite. Lawrence will tell them the creature had no chance of surviving in the outside world. The literature is unanimous, every known case confirms it: the fate of the attacker is to die with its host. This knowledge does not stop the seven incurables from punching themselves in the stomach at night or from pinching their flesh in the hope of injuring the interloper within. Nor do these simple measures preclude others of spectacular futility, like making themselves vomit and then searching the toilet bowl for traces of tiny white crustaceans.

'I heard they pulled one from a man's stomach. Thirty centimetres.'

'When I go to bed, it feels like they're climbing up my esophagus.'

'I don't see how I can keep eating. I'll never swallow anything again. Never again.'

'I can't stop seeing its pale, slimy back. And those legs!'

'Stop, I can't take it. Just don't think about it.'

Like every other facet of their lives, their insomnia is collective. One night they discover they can no longer withstand the pins and needles in their veins. They come down from their bedrooms and meet outside, at Alex's burial site. Suddenly they are shivering. They imagine they hear whispers, murmurs, something moving through the curtain of foliage. Invisible insects dart all around; the river roars. Night is every bit as alive as day.

Stretched out on the ground, they defy the world to consume them. Some bury themselves under shovelfuls of earth, leaving only their heads above ground, quietly begging the maggots to eat them if they can. But after a while they start clawing at the topsoil, until they finally pull themselves out from the earth, panting and victorious. Others let dragonflies settle on their arms, shoulders, and heads, until someone else comes by to blow them away. They are so nervous and tired. It may be a collective hallucination when a long-haired naked woman emerges from the torrent and lays her spume-white body alongside theirs. *Now we are one*, she seems to say as she caresses them in turn, grazing skin and hair, gently rubbing backs, awakening desires. When they realize where she is taking them, they start to resist. They pummel her, scratch her. She just laughs. Then she sinks her teeth into their skin and squeezes their wrists with force enough to cut off the blood flow. None can say for sure whether they are dreaming or awake. But in the end there is nothing so satisfying as an indelible pain that annihilates everything, and they know long before they see her return to the water whence she came that they have lost their bet.

They know it is her scream that rings out whenever rain falls in Shivering Heights.

At daybreak they find August, the oldest member of their group, lying in agony in the grass under pounding rain. He is curled up in a fetal position, holding his stomach with both hands. His eyes are rolled back in his head; his unnaturally stiff legs thrash against the ground.

Nearby, a container of water purifier lies on its side. It is empty. He has ingested the whole bottle.

They all have the same look – eyes wide, fists in front of mouths – as they stare. August quakes and moans. They wonder what to do. They could take him to Lawrence, force him to swallow charcoal capsules, beg him not to die. But maybe the parasite's vile legs are at this very moment performing their final reflexive kicks under the effect of the chemicals. Maybe he has found the trick to expel them, to take them with him.

It's not as if they can leave him alone. But they can't save him either.

Soon they start dying in rapid succession.

They, the six survivors.

The five.

The four.

As they perish, one after another, they'll bury their dead in the ground or throw them in the river. Never have their surroundings been so alive. The water rumbles like an undernourished stomach. The froth on the surface of the pallid whirlpools is the spitting image of the clouds. Birds squawk and lunge skyward. Mosquitoes plow along like tiny zeppelins, surrounded by other unnamed insects. Such abundance of fauna, ignored all these years. They make a funeral pyre for the fourth corpse. It takes all day to get it burning in this damp air. Eyes on the flames, they brave the stench of burning flesh, hoping to see a crablike creature wriggling as it burns. By disposing of the dead, they seek the consolation of crushing one's enemies. They want to believe they are winning. In the ashes of the fourth one they find no shells, only fragments of bone, which bring to mind the particles they ingest with each deep breath. They cough. Bring hands to throats.

They're ensnared.

From the cabin, Lawrence watches them shovelling ashes into the river, then savagely beating the air with the shovel to chase the clouds of grey dust. From time to time, tears roll down their cheeks. He had hoped to ease their suffering, at least a little. But the sight of their rage as they incinerate their dead makes him wonder whether it was all for naught. Why help a few human beings among the glut of corpses that is on its way? Why try to appease the unappeasable? Maybe, before this last gasp of a dying civilization, there is simply nothing to be done. Exhaustion gnaws at him, the desire to give it all up steals over him.

Then he watches them topple over, and get up again, and keep on working. They have such need of tenderness.

So he gets back to washing their clothes, changing their sheets, preparing medications and meals. He sweeps up the feathers they have shed and brushes their dry skin, thin hair, and iridescent scales. Their stores of food are running very low. But only four remain. One refuses to eat. In a few days all will have succumbed to the epidemic. Then he'll leave Shivering Heights for the beleaguered metropolis. If the circumstances haven't changed, and if he takes sufficient precautions, perhaps he'll manage to bring a new cohort of the dying here, to help them live out their final days in a blanket of human warmth, far from the bedlam of the cities. Sometimes, before they squeeze out their last breaths, the men and women afflicted by the catastrophe shake his hand with a surprising vigour. He wants to believe there is solace in this hand of his. When one of them comes to him, ready to set out on their final journey, he tries to channel all his powers of comfort into his palm, before the current running through him disappears, before the energy he conducts dissipates, before the electric concentration of life gives way to a feeble death rattle.

These people too will know this peace.

These four.

These three.

These two.

⚘

It's said the sky is blue and its light is what colours the water. But in this place, the misty air is fogged with greens and greys, hues running the gamut from matte to fluorescent. Hidden beneath the river's glimmering surface are countless creatures and an unprecedented threat born of recent climate change and millennia of evolution.

Seemingly oblivious to it all, the two remaining humans run as fast as they can along the banks of the raging river. Sometimes, when their focus is sharp, something unprecedented happens. Their feet leave the earth and, for a moment or two, they float, suspended in the air, ten centimetres off the ground. In this way they move forward, a metre or three, only to fall to the earth again. It doesn't stop them from trying afresh, again and again. The mother helps her son with a series of affectionate gestures. Wipes the dirt from his arms when he falls, runs alongside him while he gets moving again.

Lawrence stares in amazement. Every hair on his body bristles with joy, and his fists clench in hope each time they take flight.

'Keep going,' he says. 'Breathe! Flap your arms!'

Uncertainly, chaotically, their bodies rise. From time to time, when they attain a certain height and enter the flight path of dragonflies, Lawrence can see them growing lighter: they smile sweetly, blink more slowly.

Then they stop losing elevation. At first they glide in circles, above the ground, jerking like wounded birds. Lawrence watches, riveted. The world is no longer quite the same. The rain keeps swelling the foul river waters; the sky is still alive with biohazard colours – yet there they are: mother and son. They're flying. They start off in single file, then go side by side. They seem to communicate silently. In a single movement they break through the invisible wall separating the cabin from the rest of the world. They glide over the river's thundering torrents; the boy glances at the water's surface and then climbs a little higher, and soon they both disappear into the treetops across the water. Lawrence watches, enraptured. He is now the last man here.

He listens to the roaring river and the gusts of the wind that make the leaves whoosh and rattle the shutters. It's the wind after the storm. He is well and truly alone. Isolated amid the crows and maples and pines, the insects and billions of parasite eggs, biding their time, carried along by the river.

He takes one last look at the cabin, then slides into the water. The time has come to get back to wilder times.

SHALL WE GATHER
Sue Sinclair

The flood is not mine to suffer but only to dabble
my fingers in, skimming the rim of its shameless silvery waste,
touching the hem of its robe. It shines like grass,
like a grown-over dumpsite, holy, holy, holy. This is a new kind
of incarnation, pressing up against the houses, creating
new belief systems. The putrid scents that drifted through town
from what seemed like elsewhere now cling to our clothes.
It's time. Does every dawn radiate in some sense? For how long?
You can see it, the shift in theology; even the reflections
of the clouds have changed. A meniscus of light quivers around us,
barely holding itself together. The river's current reproduces itself
in the body as adrenalin. What has happened to us that immediacy
feels like an out-of-body experience? Pull your hand out
of the river, friend, no more gathering-at, not on this bank:
rebuilding isn't a twenty-first-century option. Come now, let's go.

SPECIES MADE EXTINCT BY HUMAN ACTIVITIES

Tiffany Morris

> *(Mistranslations from Wikipedia articles in the title category)*

I. Feather

The bird is invisible, often found in forests.
They grow on tall trees that
eat a lot of fruit and speak
the native language.

The trees are covered with feathers:
feathers do not change
over time.
The majority of them are in life
to protect it.
With his eye for the blind,
he is best known for collecting
the bones,
mimic[king] the cold of other birds,
and various messages from the sky.

In winter, small plants become large
and white,
spread from ear to ear.

II. Fur

There is more than the old bones
and cloud records;
a link to the precious fruit-
fruit, eaten with flowers.

The wild cat was confronted
by the threat of predators:
the sound of rumbling noise
and a lot of fire
slowly moving in the contours
of the ocean.

When the grass, trees, and reindeer
seemed to disappear,
he fell into a storm.

III. Scale

This is the last line
of dangerous animals.
They think you're playing with toy
bone fragments and oil,
the oil, in a flame of fire.

They jumped on the
fading of the day
looking for fresh food
and water:
the look is long
and lacks colour.

The cause of
the accident is unknown:
these giant valleys
are loving and fearful.

I STILL WANT EYELID BEES
Nikki Reimer

'it's cloying, but I like it'

how many lawyers have to set themselves on fire
before we start to *take* climate change/seriously

how many dead lawyers do I gotta fellate to
get some renewable energy strategies around here?

cancel me, father, for I have sinned
this is my twelfth confession
and/or
I'm 'sad' about 'mass species death' but I 'still use plastic strips'
to 'wax my back mole'
and/or
can we widen the focus a bit here?
and/or
I'm 'lonely'
I'm 'late-cusp Gen X'
I'm 'sincerely apathetic'
bring me all your eyelid bees
let them feast on my globular warming tears
Oh petroleum, you're the top predator now[1]
Majestic apex of the patch
bring me all your eyelid bees
and set yourself on fire.

---

1. Neko Case / Paul Rigby, 'Dirty Diamond' lyrics © Kobalt Music Publishing Ltd., Peermusic Publishing.

ONLY THE SUN
Emily Schultz

Who will notice when this leaf is gone?
It is only a leaf,
tiny, trembling, green; tomorrow's auburn.
No one will know. Only the bird will know.

Who will notice when this love is gone?
It is only a love,
a ghost thing with no edges or shape.
No one will know. Only I will know.

Who will notice when this song is gone?
It is only a song,
one sound set beside another like a pair of shoes.
No one will know. Only we will know.

Who will notice when the sun is gone?
It is only a sun,
a hole of gold burned into an endless sky.
No one will know. Only the dark will know.

26
Kunjana Parashar

In the 1990s, diclofenac was used to treat cattle diseases. Many vultures started dropping dead after feeding on the medicated carcasses: *Gyps bengalensis, G. Indicus,* and *G. Tenuirostris* – they took a hit so bad that later the Parsis planned to build vulture aviaries for the traditional departure of their dead. I was born in that decade – somewhere around the confirmed end of Javan tigers. Since my birth, there are others who have gone extinct – birds, civets, rhinos. And yet, countless anurans hide in the Western Ghats. Turn this shola, peatland, lateritic plateau – and you will find a species still willing to live, shy only of the blessed grace of taxonomy. When my mother asks how I want to celebrate my birthday this year, I say, *quietly.*

Barry Pottle, *Under the Scope, Micro*, 2019, digital photograph.

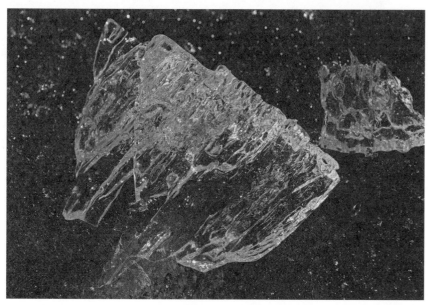

Barry Pottle, *Hopeful Antibodies*, 2020, digital photograph.

Adam Gunn, *Ruin Value*, 2019, oil on wood panel, 27.5" x 53"

National Iranian Drilling, (MOBIL), Ahvaz M.I.S.Road, Kooye Mellat, 61635 Iran

Eshrat Erfanian, *Tres-pass 1*, 2005–2007.

Eshrat Erfanian, *Tres-pass 3*, 2005–2007.

Gaye Jackson, *Erratic #4*, 2011.

Gaye Jackson, *Erratic #8*, 2013.

PLANET AT THE CROSSROADS

Christine Leclerc

Originally published on Dec. 5, 2019, for Ricochet Media.

On Dec. 6, the crosswalk near Nuevos Ministerios metro station in Madrid may become one of the most photographed crosswalks on earth. If the city's Sept. 27 climate strike is anything to go by, we can expect thousands to flood the area. The Spanish cosmopolis, now more cosmopolitical than usual with tens of thousands here for the UN's Conference of Youth 15 (COY15) and Conference of Parties 25 (COP25) to advance climate action, is launching crosswalks like this into the global spotlight.

While anxieties about the lack of progress on decarbonization increase with each annual Conference of the Parties, there are signs that times are changing, thanks in no small part to our resolute and vocal youth. My home country of Canada, for example, has declared a climate emergency. In recent days, the EU has also declared an emergency. This is in addition to over a thousand cities that have issued declarations, many of which have established decarbonization pathways.

Relentless global climate strikes demonstrate strong political will for bold climate action among we-the-peoples — the ones to whom heads of government are accountable. Perplexingly, despite this global mandate, many nations continue to stall or send mixed messages about their commitment to neutralizing the climate crisis and upholding Indigenous rights, the right to a healthy environment, and the right to a livable future.

However much disagreement there may be among and within nations, there is something that unites us, and that is the crosswalk. All nations have crosswalks, or concepts like it, to tell us whose turn it is to go. Crosswalks around the world may differ in design, but the values they balance are remarkably similar. In the case of crosswalks that bisect roadways, we can see the interplay of values such as mobility and public safety.

Crosswalks are physical installations to be sure, but they are also signed spaces interpreted by those who flow through them. They save lives because, from a young age, most of us are taught how to use them as pedestrians, and later in life how to avoid hitting others while driving. When we travel to other countries we recognize and use crosswalks. And perhaps most importantly, there is no place where people who do not want to stop for pedestrians can hit them with impunity. These pieces of civic infrastructure are as universal as the values of security and autonomy. What I suggest is that crosswalks, and the bylaws that establish them, are so consistently applied around the world, including in marine settings, that they operate as an international law would, except with tens of thousands of courts to apply the law, instead of one.

The climate crisis is killing people whose communities are being destroyed by extreme weather, sea-level rise, and wildfires. There are also less sensational but equally tragic deaths, like that of the man who tries to drive his snowmobile across a lake that no longer freezes to its previous depth, or the elder who cannot afford air conditioning on her fixed income and passes in a lengthy heatwave.

Unlike jaywalking or reckless driving, one needn't act to put one's life at risk when it comes to the climate. For now, simply living puts us at risk, not just as individuals but as a species. Yet critics of global democratic governance argue against straightforward measures to ensure rapid decarbonization, such as an end to fossil-fuel subsidies, a fully costed global price on carbon, and land-use rules to protect biodiversity.

So, all we need is a global patchwork of ambitious bylaws to address these issues, right? While cities are in many ways leading the charge on decarbonizing their operations, significant greenhouse-gas emissions occur outside of cities, so a more universal instrument is needed to actualize our shared values of interdependence with other species and a livable future.

Lest you doubt our ability to value other species, not just as edibles or wearables but as beings whose lived lives are critical to our own survival and who are inherently worthy of love and respect, consider the response to recent bushfires that have put koalas at risk of extinction. People living in places far from Australia are making mittens to help injured koalas heal from their burns. This is just one of many examples of humans reaching out to members of another species to help them recover from the harms of climate change.

When it comes to greenhouse-gas emissions and the destruction of Earth's carbon sinks, we've been driving too fast. Heads of government have thus far failed to act on the fact that we are about to drive off a cliff. Indeed, to avoid runaway climate change, emissions must peak in 2020. Now is the time to stop and put in a global crosswalk.

REVOLUTION
Jessica Magonet

I've always thought of it as an affront,
as the place where two waves crash
and fall

but as I ride down the Bow River pathway
and watch bicycle wheels spin
I wonder if revolution is more like turning away
from where you are
to circle
back again

at the environmental conference
the psychologist says breaking addiction takes time

the man from the premier's office
asks if we are prepared
to make the sacrifice

I think of my plane tickets to New Orleans
of the crude oil
on my hands

the retired teacher tells us
she brought her students to the woods
so they would know
this too is home

Naomi Klein wrote a leap manifesto
but maybe there is no place to jump to
or from

maybe there is just this place
right here
and the way we must begin to turn around it

like Sufi poets
kissing the earth
with our twirling gowns

HOW TO FIND YOUR WAY IN STRATHCONA COUNTY
Curtis LeBlanc

No frost can stay on the steel or chrome,
warmed by the volumes of raw
and seething oil, the smell of which
is nondescript to those who find their way
by the pale blue light of the mercury-vapour lamps,
glowing by the hundreds on Refinery Row.
Drive until you can count them
through the cylinders and smoke.
Go until you see the stacks, small fires
poised high into the night.
These are the stars that guide the North.

REFRAIN
Hari Alluri
   after Suheir Hammad

hum is sanskrit
for *we*

hum rising
hum crest

hum descended

hum falling

enemies tongue folded letters elbows shoulder blades hum

unravel shells geometry orchards labour coriander melodies torn

hum ligaments
almost connected
knees unbound from reverence toes away from pulses clenched

hum wounds
hum open
hum salt water
rushing to tighten skin blood
rushing to feed the earth
unparallel streams

hum count the dead hum shop on saturday
behind closed doors hum wasn't my decision
out on the block hum say not enough
hum why don't you hum
if you so brave
hum do it all

   to preserve
create   destroy
   to preserve

humaara faith
the cycle perfect

hum pray
to be wrong

hum tire
against snow

hum armour
against home

hum cracks trying to join voices from bodies
razed in brackets (all else road)

I AM WRITING A SPELL FOR YOUR NERVOUS SYSTEM
Anna Swanson

and hiding it in a poem.
I know you're trying to stitch

the world back together
while it breathes and keeps

breaking. Like you. Another
heatwave, hurricane. Grief

gurgles like a sump pump.
The Arctic on fire. Thirsty birds

of industry, mouthing
dry wells. Bulldozers

in the olive grove. Prehensile
suits in a sealed building,

deciding who deserves
to be a person. Baby monitors

tuned to the evening news.
Geologic time is breathing

hard. Your nerves: clenched
shut like barnacles and still

flinching. I am casting a road
out of the city. Stop waiting

for CNN to self-soothe.
Stop memorizing formulas

for herbal abortion, just
in case, even though

some futures are no longer
unimaginable. Here

is a highway that vanishes
behind you like wet footprints.

Gravel pullout, the rule
of three boulders across

an unmarked road. The car door
closing with a reverse bang,

retracting into itself
the existence of cars.

Because you are in a poem,
rusted mile-markers appear

only for as long as you walk
the dirt road toward them.

Now a marshy spot, now
lily pads, now wooden pallets

thrown down for you to cross.
Labrador tea and pitcher plants

flanking a narrow trail, and
wasn't it ever only this?

An opening in the trees.
Worn stones sloping down

to the flickering mirror of a pond.
Step out of the idea of clothes

into a shallow dive.
Fingertip-to-fingertip

with your reflection – and
gone. A beat later, slick

and blinking, as if from a dark
room: somersault, scissor kick,

glide. Your body diamond-tipped,
a stylus polishing a groove.

Practise this skin. A dark map
back here, sparking, neural.

When it is time, walk up out
of the pond, dripping with

what made you. The world
leans down over cupped palms

to blow you dry. When you are
ready for clothes to exist,

clothes. The path winks
into existence before you.

Eventually you think,
I had a car. Onward,

the messy heartbeat
of the world. And whatever

work you have to do,
you begin again.

ERASURE: A RESPONSE TO 'MUSÉE DES BEAUX ARTS' AND SUFFERING

Yvonne Blomer and Jenna Butler

I.

A Seam-Ripped Rendition of 'Musée des Beaux Arts' by W. H. Auden, by Jenna Butler

About suffering they were never wrong, / The Old Masters, those straw men of Parliament Hill, tilting at windmills in the shape of pumpjacks, pipelines, Alberta's backhanded shadow. **How well they understood / Its human position: how it takes place** at night on Wet'suwet'en land, legalized slink of gas hunger on unceded territory. UNDRIP, Coastal Gaslink; *Canada, brandish your Reconciliation as what it is:* false flag, smokescreen. **While someone else is eating or opening a window or just walking dully along;** night-vision goggles and automatic weapons, militarized police in Unist'ot'en in the early morning. Muzzle the media, blind the lenses: lived experience sees no apology. **How, when the aged are reverently, passionately waiting / For the miraculous birth,** Canada Pension and Old Age Security, **there must always be / Children who did not specially want it to happen, skating / On a pond at the edge of the wood:** tripping gaily around the methane bubbles, the buckling permafrost. What call to childhood, this – the lakes gagging with blue-green algae, the good clean water trucked south to the States. **They never forgot / That even the dreadful martyrdom must run its course,** cost-benefit analysis picked out in monarchs and rainforest, wildfires, eucalyptus groves. Tahlequah's dirge for a thousand miles.

Anyhow in a corner, some untidy spot / Where the dogs go on with their doggy life and the torturer's horse / Scratches its innocent behind on a tree, that's where you'll trip over a cabal of politicians, heads-in-sand, rank festivus of backslapping and oil goggles. **In Breughel's Icarus, for instance: how everything turns away / Quite leisurely from the disaster;** *and why not, eh, Boomers?* As long as there are doctors enough for hordes of retirees, why lose sleep over Conservative boondoggling, the missile click of an oil-slick War Room locking on target? **The ploughman may / have heard the splash, the forsaken cry, / But for him it was not an important failure.** After all, we are only women left to rot along a northern highway. We are only children outed by our teachers. We are Alloura Wells and Julie Berman, every scooped teen and starlight tour. **The sun shone / As it had to on the white legs disappearing into the green / Water,** onto the white guys constantly falling up, into Stanford (*after all, he's a good swimmer*), into the White House (*not impeached, but innocent*), and if you don't see race, then I can guarantee you're not coloured. The self-censuring fear of buying a new car, moving to a better neighbourhood, *being a Black man in America.* **And the expensive delicate ship that must have seen / Something amazing, a boy falling out of the sky,** but not the girl he took with him because *she was dressed like that and she was asking for it,* that ship **had somewhere to get to and sailed calmly on.**

About Suffering, by Yvonne Blomer

after 'Musée des Beaux Arts' by W. H. Auden and 'When it comes to hypocrisy Canadian leaders have reached a new low,' Bill McKibben, The Guardian, *Feb 5, 2020*

About suffering   about suffering   about
suffering they have never   known
Those **Old Masters**   nor the one percent   nor the world's
leaders   locked in their safe rooms with water

and oxygen hoarded   **About suffering**
how much they misunderstand   their old
ideas   barbaric as the RCMP arresting Wet'suwet'en in the dark
where cameras cannot see ·   **The Old Masters**
how well they understand their own **position** –
No country would find 173 billion barrels of oil in the ground
        and leave them there, says Prime Minister Trudeau –
and think their view is   humanity's
How everyday and how **reverently** we pray   to **suffering**
for it brings shoes and new clothes
                    monarch butterflies killed so we can eat avocados
Refugees sent back to unstable countries so they can be shot
(by American rifles?)
About suffering   **The Old Masters** know well
                            as makers of such suffering
(but ahh   but ohh   this poem – the Master Poet Auden speaks of
Icarus   a tiny afterthought   sidebar   like the bee hummingbird
or the Vancouver Island marmot   endlings)
What do the great Masters care
of animals when they are artmaking?   Beavers
for hats   koalas' burnt tails   and coal mining prevails
paintbrushes   of badger   hog bristle   sable
The Old Masters suffer   weep
for the prize   recognition   while a child is stolen
raised for war   and young Icarus falls
    everything turns away   says Auden
            while **the dog**
is missing an eye   **the torturer's horse** has a bloat to its belly
from plastic and Styrofoam,   a pipe runs through the **pond**
and children can't skate on water that never freezes

and children   who did not specially want it to happen nonetheless
will not make middle age   food rare in a land without bees
where swarms of locusts plague   fill the air

and Icarus plunges   he plunges   in a quiet corner
while everything dies
or **turns away**   **leisurely**   our pace toward change
while Icarus   Icarus

                                       falls
into a too-warm sea   suffering terribly there

II.

The Old Masters
             those straw men of Parliament Hill
             tilting at windmills in the shape of pumpjacks

Those **Old Masters**
             locked in their safe rooms with water
and oxygen hoarded

or just walking dully along, night-vision goggles and automatic
    weapons
militarized police in Unist'ot'en in the early morning

                       About suffering
how much they misunderstand   their old
ideas   barbaric as the RCMP arresting Wet'suwet'en in the dark
where cameras can't see

On a pond at the edge of the wood, tripping gaily around the methane
    bubbles
the buckling permafrost

**Anyhow in a corner, some untidy spot / Where the dogs go on with
their doggy life and the torturer's horse / Scratches its innocent
behind on a tree**

everything turns away
while the dog
is missing an eye **the torturer's horse** has a bloat to its belly
from plastic and Styrofoam, a pipe runs through the pond
and children can't skate on water that never freezes

it was not an important failure. After all, we are only women left to rot
along a northern highway. We are only children outed by our teachers

and children **who did not specially want it to happen** nonetheless
will not make middle age food rare in a land without bees
where plague fill(s) the air

**The sun shone / As it had to on the white legs disappearing into the
green / Water** onto the white guys constantly falling up, into the
White House
and if you *don't see race*, then I can guarantee you're not coloured

and Icarus plunges he plunges in a quiet corner
while everything dies
or turns away

**And the expensive delicate ship that must have seen / Something
amazing, a boy** falling out of the sky, but not the girl he took with him
because *she was dressed like that and she was asking for it*, that ship **had
somewhere to get to and sailed**

leisurely
our pace toward change

while Icarus Icarus
falls
into a too-warm sea suffering terribly there

III.

        pumpjacks

those **Old Masters**

vision goggles and automatic weapons

Unist'ot'en in the early morning
Wet'suwet'en in the dark

methane bubbles, the buckling permafrost
a pipe   through the pond
and **children** can't skate on water that never freezes

only women left to rot
children
will not make middle age

        while everything dies
or turns away

            falls
into a too-warm sea   suffering terribly

Kevin Adonis Browne, 'Decapitated Palms' from *The Coast* series, 2017 (Trinidad).

Kevin Adonis Browne, 'King Tide' from *The Coast* series, 2017 (Trinidad).

THIS POEM IS A DEAD ZONE
Krishnakumar Sankaran

The ocean is suffocating.

– Dr. Bastien Queste

(UEA's School of Environmental Sciences)[1]

Here is a place you walk into backwards,
hands held out before you to push back
the greying sky. One leg tense with the burden
of earth, the other, a jaunty angle
sinking in the bioluminescent green.
Here is a wind out of water, a transparent sheet
swaddling you back into the freedom offered
by thrashing four limbs, by holding your mouth
perfectly ajar like a grotto spitting bubbles.
Screw your eyes shut against the pressure
of lines in the floating page receding
above you. When fish pass you by,
measure your pulse by their dying breaths.
When bone-white coral scrapes your vertebrae,
remember the practised smile of the skull
on every sign that warned, 'DANGER.'
When the bed breathes floating sand displaced
by your settling in, dream of nights
when stars were falling dust.

---

1. University of East Anglia. 'Growing "dead zone" confirmed by underwater robots in the Gulf of Oman.' ScienceDaily. www.sciencedaily.com/releases/2018/04/180427113251.htm (accessed May 28, 2020).

MAKE A LIVING

Allison Cobb

To make a living: 'alive,
not dead,' the dictionary
definition says, from an Old
English word: 'to be left;
to live, of fire: to burn'
from an even older root –
'to stick, adhere,' and with
that sense of hanging
on, each morning's pre-
work nauseous darkness,
exhaustion deep enough
to snuff out fire
from eyes beside the freeway
holding out a sign, I look
and look away, I pay
a month of groceries
for boots I hope
will bring me
back to life – they don't.
They hurt, a hurt
that burns through
tissue to tendon
or bone, slow-fired
nerve fibres sparking.

🌱

My love
asks if I've seen a living
tree hold fire –
it burns alive

for years, how
an embryo's pulse
of blood carves grooves
in soft skull bones, often
mistaken later for fractures –
the break of beating
life – not
a metaphor, but for the ways
medicine sickens
the body in the startle
response of late capital. Trees
don't burn alive for years,
at least Google gives me
no evidence of this, but
coal seams do, and tires,
and money burns its
need inside
the four-year-old whose
eyes aglow with TV light says
Mommy, mommy, can I have
that magic talking grill??!!
The World Trade Center burned
for a hundred days, a funeral
pyre of empire – which means
a span of earth and all
who dwell there subject
to another's power – drifting
molecules through our nostrils
down into lungs to add
to the blood's toxic cargo.

✤

I love you, I said
with eternal flame
like Baba Gurgur,
the oil field in Iraq,
alive with fire
four thousand years
or more, no human
remembers, long believed
the world's largest
lake of fossil life, its
dagger of fire said
to favour pregnant
worshippers with
baby boys. By you
I meant my love. By love
I meant I'm glad,
my love, you survived
being female, and queer,
the force of hands
and sticks on skin,
and forced inside, and then
erased by those
who birthed you. I'm glad,
I said, which comes from
the root for 'shine,' as in
alight with the fire
of joy, that we can live
in love in the factory
farm of capital as cattle,
which first meant any form
of property, as opposed to
debt, which means to take
endlessly, I said, I'm glad.
I'm glad I survived the burning,

falling towers. I lived
in a fog of privilege,
my whole life blurred
by a belief in my own
exceptional security
and the violent fathers
who nurtured me. I know
now what it is to hold
the burn of terror –
from 'to tremble' –
to extinguish the myth
of safety, to choose
to live in the flame light anyway.

SAFETY NET
Yohani Mendis

I'm on vacation in a place where two languages feuded, took up arms, and began a war.

It is 7 a.m. Sri Lanka time, and despite the jet lag, I'm playing tourist in my birth country on this double-decker vessel, its side emblazoned with the logo of a spouting whale and 'Dilshan's Tours' in jolly red font. A headcount by the captain – probably Dilshan himself – up front, as I follow his bobbing eyes around deck, tells me two things: I'm the only brown-skinned passenger on this boat and this tour is overbooked. My outlier presence is zeroed in on by a latecomer, the spokesman of a big-hats-and-sunblock-laden entourage from a wealthier Asian country. Waving emphatically in my direction, he laments to the captain, 'You can't give our reserved seats to your friends, it's not fair.' I would like to tell him that a fair arrangement could be made with a few choice words before a final 'man overboard!' settles his overcrowding concern. I glance toward my left and meet my boyfriend's green eyes, his entreating look, as if to say, 'We're on holiday; let's not make a scene?'

I've said time and again that these yearly trips around the island are for his benefit, but that's a lie and he knows it. Each time, I am on a mission to anchor as many roots as possible to compensate for decades of living abroad. Leaving it up to the captain to sort out today's special passenger, I confront the hypnotic gaze of the waves rocking the sides of the boat, the Indian Ocean sighing beneath our feet. My father's folk, the Karava clan, were coastal traders in the seventeenth century and likely among the first southerners to sight the Portuguese ships, the first in a steady drain of colonizers.

The motor sputters to life and tugs us out of the dock, away from the smell of dying sea creatures floundering in nets. Down at the shore, fishermen perch on stilts in the water, their sarongs hitched up wiry thighs. I have read that nowadays this tactic is less about catching fish than it is foreigners, the more abundant and less slippery fellows. Sure enough, a pair of bohemian-clad paparazzi run out from under the tree cover, hand-in-hand into the low tide, and one deposits a tip into the model's weathered palms. The photos will resurface in their globetrotter-touting blogs, entered into photo contests that feature fading world traditions. In these times of dynamite fishing and deep-sea trawling, they are the stilt fishermen's most consistent catch. As our boat gathers speed, the men grow smaller and smaller until the expanse of water swallows them.

I'm not entirely sure what I'm doing on this whale-watching tour, buying into the sanitized stories of paradise that travel agencies sell, when I could be spending the precious minutes in the hill capital of Kandy with my parents, recent retirees and returnees to their birthplace after decades of working in the Middle East. The captain is frantically talking on his phone, getting a tip-off from another tour boat nearby on the whereabouts of whales. Speed picks up, cameras at the ready, and with a sinking feeling I notice another dozen boats like ours appearing out of nowhere to converge. The captain's yells for everyone to remain seated have the opposite effect; almost everyone rushes over to the side of the alleged sighting, tilting the deck. I silently pray that Big Hat Sunblock Man does not know how to swim. The commotion dissipates almost as soon as it began – a false alarm. My Very Canadian Boyfriend is visibly distressed at how the animals' boundaries aren't respected and I tell him there are no such regulations here, whether animals or people.

As the boat cruises farther out to sea, the crewmen start serving up cups of black tea and *pol sambol* sandwiches. One of them singles me out for a chat, sidling over to my seat. Sinhala is becoming a tattered robe I wear for identification when the need arises. The Indo-Aryan dialect feels stilted and in parts broken from too many years spent living in various countries and no one to speak with. No. That's partly a lie. My parents, worried my English skills would fail me in the big world if they spoke or taught their mother tongue at home, steered clear of it. They had a change of heart by the time my adult teeth had fully grown in, hastily packing my brother and me off to Sinhala classes thrice a week after school. Unbeknownst to them, a pretty girl at the British private school I attended had kindly pointed out that I came from the country of housemaids. A month into the classes, my twelve-year-old self loudly declared that I did not want to learn the language of housemaids anymore. That put an end to my parents' linguistic experiment.

My sad 'Singlish' doesn't dissuade the crewman from chatting in a decisively in-group manner. He asks where I live, and when I say Canada his brows furrow like a dark cloud over his eyes.

'Lots of Tamils there, no?' The inability to exit a boat in the same way one would an unsavoury dinner party dawns on me. I look away and scan the horizon for a sea mammal that isn't there.

Fifteen years earlier, a new species of whale was sighted in these waters. Once an unassuming fishermen's bay, Mirissa now boasts a myriad of gaudily painted tour boats, surf shacks, and questionable bed and breakfasts. 'The Colonial Experience Resthouse, open for business,' I read from a sign on our drive back from the tour, which had ended an hour earlier than estimated. Not that either of us minded much; the seaward excursion had devolved into a race of motorboats charging time and again toward grey specks they told us were whales.

We spend the rest of the day in Galle town with Elephant House iced lollies dripping down our hands.

To my surprise, at the maritime museum I get free entry when I speak in Sinhala, the attendant nodding approval at this exemplar diaspora. He explains that since I have brought a *suddha* with me, my admittance is on the house. We wander through the partially open–roofed halls with a million shards of light falling through the cracks, musing at wreckage dealt to the first colonial ships by the Indian sea.

We step outside, climbing atop the fort's south-facing ledge. Giddy with salty breeze and the ocean ablaze with fleeting light, I tease that we should quit our jobs in Toronto and move here. The war that drove my family, like so many others, out of this place is over. I could get a diving licence, disappearing for days into this aqueous, wordless world. I could conveniently forget the reasons why my Sinhalese, island-loving parents left it all behind. Reasons that include but are not limited to: burnt bodies strung from lampposts, weekly bombings in Colombo, food rationing, nuns demanding bribes for preschool admission, free speech–stifling spies, fat cats carving chunks out of a country and selling them to foreign buyers for a song and all the while the coral beds are crumbling, turning a sickly sepia monochrome, and no one sees the loss as it happens –

Just like that, the ephemeral light is gone, replaced by a dull crimson splayed across the horizon.

'It's a great place for a holiday, love. Now, don't get me wrong, but I feel trapped here,' says a voice that sounds a thousand miles away. I give my boyfriend an incomprehensible stare.

'You speak the language,' he says, 'But if I was on my own, I'd be helpless in getting around. Or looked at like I'm a walking money bag.' He chuckles, before asking my help in buying rambutan from a street vendor at local prices.

I'd forgotten to get a local chip for my phone at the airport, but the old Dutch lighthouse guides us back to where we left our car.

We return to our beachfront hotel just after six. Flanking the entrance to the lobby are two Kandyan drummers who thunder up a song and dance routine each time a car rolls up the porte cochère. Half-dressed women and men in every shade of sunburn saunter past us in the direction of the poolside bar, buffet, and ocean. Our bellies remind us that it's been a long time since lunch, and we beeline for dinner. I join the hungry queue at the hopper station, watching a weary cook crack eggs into the swirling crepe-like batter. At long last, my turn comes. I place my order in Sinhala and her eyes briefly light up before asking where I am from.

'Kandy, hill country,' I say with a smile and ask her the same.

SPAWNING GROUNDS
Isabella Wang

1. Sandcastle Bucket

This fable I grew up hearing that told of a time when the sea
swept to shore all of its fishes. From the bluefin tuna off Scarborough
to the mackerels migrating off the coast, and what's left of wild sturgeon
near Brescia, northern Italy. Where sinkholes formed, where they
were met with obstructions, and where the tide began to retreat,
the fish cannot get back. Along one shore, a child came
with a sandcastle bucket, grabbed the fish by the handfuls, and carried
them back to where they were released into the waters.
All this time, a bystander watched. They asked the child, *Why bother?*
There are so many of them. To this, the child replied,
At least I'm doing something. Hurry. The next time the sea turns again,
there will be no more fish left to pick up.

2. Listen

A plastic bag pirouettes on the road. Watch how it heaves
and falls in the air, clear as diatoms, like jellyfish in the water –
formation driven by the motor of vehicles pumping 250 mph, the wind
blowing east, and no one picks it up. Twenty-five plastic cups, a nylon sack,
and two flip-flops are not enough for conservation researchers
to determine the cause of death, the sperm whale was too well-decayed.
A carcass washed ashore at a Southeast Sulawesi provincial park:
a signal, as villagers read. An innuendo seemingly
to invite the words, come,
butcher me. So they do.

3. Shoreline

Sixty million cigarette butts currently clogging our oceans but we don't
think of the watershed as a massive ashtray. More than plastic water
bottles, more than straws, dislodged caps, and unlike plastic, filters
can't be picked up. What's biodegradable disintegrates, what's
disintegrated carries into rivers by rain, arsenic, nicotine, lead,
into oceans by waves. Our ecosystem into waterways, making a return
back to our bodies.

4. Spawning Grounds

A female salmon by intuition returns to her prenatal stream carrying
the weight of up to 3,000 eggs. These, she will climb to deposit
in the hollows of gravel and sediment above falls, packed between
fresh-water riverbeds, but to be met along the way by the dam
on Muskrat Falls off Labrador, the Keeyask dam on the Nelson River,
ninety-three square kilometres of hydro across boreal lands,
snow forests liquefied where a common spawning ground
resides for the wild fish being met with the Site C Dam
though BC – 128 kilometres of river flooded, the Peace River
a reservoir, an Indigenous burial ground and home
to one hundred endangered species. In the south, seventy-six killer whales
left on the brink of extinction. We erect hydro dams and rear fish
in hatcheries away from their natural habitat, bring wildlife
back into nature, nature back into industrialization: this is what
we call rewilding. The bare necessities of hatcheries strengthened
through genetic engineering, forced interbreeding, but fish that rely
on muscle memory year after year are the ones
we see failing to return.

DEBATING FOUNDATIONS
Elee Kraljii Gardiner and Andrew McEwan

It comes down to an intercession. It comes down
to exit strategies. It comes down to plain sight. It
comes down to salt-sprayed rocks. It comes down
to you, and you are alone. It comes down to the
fiction of neutrality. It comes down to birds of a
feather. It comes down to the raw materials at
hand. It comes down to fellow creatures. It comes
down to the economy. It comes down to the
wannabes and the posers. It comes down to a
feedback loop or a bottom line. It comes down to
environmental forces. It comes down to trees and
mountains. It comes down to pre-vetted entries.
It comes down to floors and dirt. It comes down
to property rights. It comes down to the maple
leaves pressed between thick pages. It comes down
to the absurdity and brutality of taxonomy. It
comes down to purple on the lee. It comes down
to folded arms, tied hands. It comes down to a
question of taste. It comes down to who wants to
win more. It comes down to fluctuating mortgage
rates. It comes down to witness credibility. It
comes down to intertidal zones. It comes down
to the nuts and bolts. It comes down to who was
here first. It comes down to working environ-
ments. It comes down to taste. It comes down to
the music of the sea. It comes down to areas of
refuge. It comes down to peaks and valleys. It
comes down to muscle flexing. It comes down to
participation, transparency, and trust. It comes
down to clusters of fireweed. It comes down to
development interests. It comes down to natural

resources. It comes down to semantics. It comes down to the last minute. It comes down to geography, not popularity. It comes down to whether or not there is a person in the poem. It comes down to the root systems that hold the soil in place to prevent soil run-off. It comes down to an exact violence. It comes down to indifference. It comes down to dim-lit shores. It comes down to liberal self-congratulation. It comes down to biotic composition. It comes down to the interests of management. It comes down to a difference of taste. It comes down to money. It comes down to the co-evolution of parasites and hosts. It comes down to chance. It comes down to echoes after twilight. It comes down to landmarks used in navigation. It comes down to the dark.

MELTWATER BASIN
Ellen Chang-Richardson

Have you ever had those dreams,
you know, those carbon-dark
sorts of dreams?

Where monsters and men made
of the same fabric move in
and out of each other, amorphic?

I've had   those sorts of dreams.
Those lamp-black
sorts of dreams.

In each one
there you are
on horseback,   bareback
from the waist up.

In each one, there you are:
astride   your shadow steed
like a legion of Kazakh kings;

damn them,
these dreams.
These gut-wrenching,
teeth-clenching,
sweaty sorts of dreams, that
melt in   to each other
profuse and confused, soporific in nature.

It's funny, these
sorts of dreams, these
burnt-sienna, lamp-flare, cotton-filled dreams.

They remind me of a time, long past
when my seas and your shores met like towers in rain,
they remind me.

Of leafy green, high golden mushroom haze;
where my lips and your limbs met
wrapped, in polyurethane.

ODE TO A COMMON NIGHTHAWK
Cory Lavender

No hawk and less and less common
        my first goatsucker
parked heedful where eagles cruise
the Mersey for smallmouth, ducklings.

Bugeater flits down oceanward drift
squeaks by on dwindling pickings.
Broad white wing patches twilit
scrawl the signature flightpath.

In this life, on repeat, Hank Williams
has asked me to hear the lonesome
whippoorwill too blue to cry.
I live in range of that nightjar

according to Peterson's field guide
but have never heard the sad fowl sing
let alone picked out its cryptic plumage
among the branches and brambles.

Petering flocks. Not even a hawk. Surely
no drainer of goat teats, a blame game
Aristotle started. Nor was it night. No.
Plenty light left to watch the odd bird bode.

TO COPE
Sâkihitowin Awâsis

it's all unseasonal rains
winter in the Great Lakes these days
in *niibin* the boreal is ablaze
the amazon and outback aflame
increasing tsunamis and earthquakes
and all we can do is yell CLIMATE CHANGE
what else do we say?
while the US keeps taking brown babies away
numbered like the West Bank
Bantustans
Japanese internment camps
Auschwitz
the Indian Act

our migration routes are older than your borders
we have cultural items older than your legal orders

this is natural law renaissance
embodying ancestors' excellence
bringing land back
on ready when RCMP attack

Unist'ot'en *bimaadiziwin*
resistance is a way of living

---

niibin: summer
bimaadiziwin: way of living

CREATION
Sâkihitowin Awâsis

do you ever feel like

no one speaks your language?

like individual actions

could never make systemic changes?

you are comprised of thousands
upon thousands
of ancestral faces

recognize
land   water   plant   food
medicine relations

we are living the stories
of our sacred places

it's what tear gas
at Standing Rock tastes like

it's your family's
illegal trapline at night

casualties of the giveaway
babies' plight

the coming together
and ground shaking

of timely   highway   blockade   vibration

          hold on
                    to thunderous emplacements

          that liberate
                    and defend creation

SNAPSHOT
Jana Prikryl

When the floods came, washing out tailors
with small square change booths whose fabric
portals never entirely seal you in in dry cleaners
it helped to have done this exercise.

The luxury of each ending's weakness
for order is the time afforded
between falls to picture what will follow.

No one seems to mind
the season at Fort Tilden stretching
to October, even right-thinking people celebrate
by turning the phone on themselves, the sea behind.

For accuracy in prophecy perhaps
it helps to be unmoved by beaches.
The digital files speak and decompose.

SNAPSHOT
Jana Prikryl

Because the needle at the top of the Chrysler Building
is visible now and then under whitecaps
slightly more of the Empire State
pokes up, like a buoy.

A coral garden Central Park
dreaming at the bottom.
Every shipwrecked cab and bus
noble in its sacrifice.

None but ethical barnacles tackle the struts of the Brooklyn Bridge
while hedonists lap the sweet water
still trapped in the pipes of Harlem walk-ups.

How pleased is the subway
to lose the distinction
of being alone in being under everything.

FORTY-NINE
Sue Goyette

The harbour didn't like being held captive by the shadows of our buildings.
We treated it well but still its dorsal fins

weakened and flopped. The tide was nothing more than
a sleepy scratch of water up over rocks

and then a yawn back down. The balls we threw to it
sank. It stopped slurping, it stopped nibbling.

It hardly growled. Some days it looked like a carpet,
other days, a flooded campsite: disks of paper plates,

lipsticked cigarette butts, the wet embers
of our vacations. What was the fun of these skyscrapers

if the only view we had was a petulant body of water?
We bought fish from the market to feed it. The older women

crocheted the most tender dialogue skimmed from our dreams,
carrying afghans by the armload down to its shore.

In this way, they invented nets and managed to catch
the grit of starlight from previous nights. With the right amount

of sugar and boiled darkness, we soon had vats
of a nectar so potent it bubbled. It wasn't that we got drunk

but forgetful and became so greedy for more, we overfished
our dreams for their tenderness. When poverty arrived,

we were down to the bones of our talk. If we rubbed
two sticks together, briefly we'd be nourished by the smell

of their wood.

FIFTY-FIVE
Sue Goyette

Our elders insisted the ocean was still there.
That we were born with a seed of it and when we spoke,

its waves pressed against our words for a further shore.
But we had let ourselves become subdivided and suburban,

buckling our talk into seatbelts, mad always for safety.
When had our schedules become the new mountains?

We were doing our best to ignore how grey our memories
were becoming, how stooped and hard of hearing our laughter was.

The ocean, apparently, was right in front of us and we were dropping
like flies. We bought the dried flower tops of our politicians'

explanations. We tuned our radios to the sunsets and downloaded
whalesong overdubbed with protest songs. Our intent was good

but with airbags. The poets rigged antennas to the antique words
of gratitude with a cayenne of the unexpected but we were tired

of the poets, they were chesterfields or they were curtains.
We wanted pure ocean podcast into our veins but tethered

while we slept. We wanted death to be a stranger we'd never have to
give directions to. We consulted the beekeepers infamous

for not getting stung but they were in a meeting with the poets.
We consulted the gamblers but they wanted to see us only to raise us

ten. Our voices were rarely coming home covered in mud anymore.

FIFTY-SIX
Sue Goyette

Filmmakers had started making films of the ocean
in 3D. Scratch-and-sniff coastal cards were sold

at lottery booths. Material for dresses was cut with the froth
of tide in mind. We had wanted the ocean to be the new

flavour, the new sound. We'd drive for miles to get a glimpse
of it because, let's face it, it revitalized the part of us

we kept rooting for, that apple seed of energy that defied
multiple-choice career options. The ocean had egged the best part

of us on. And it scared us. We never knew what it was thinking
and spent thousands on specialists who could make predictions.

And the predictions always required hard hats and building permits,
furrowed eyebrows and downward trends. Why is it so hard

to trust something that leaps, disappears, and then reappears
spouting more light? When had our hearts become badly behaved

dogs we had to keep the screen door closed to? Have you ever run
along its shore, the pant of it coming closer? And that feeling

that yipped inside of you, the Ginger Rogers of your feet, your ability
to not get caught then, yes, get soaked. Didn't you feel like it was

part of your pack? When it whistled, whatever it is in you
that defies being named, didn't that part of you perk up?

And didn't you let it tousle you to the ground,
let it clean between your ears before it left you?

Wasn't that all right? That it left you? That we all will?

NOTES FROM A SMALL PLACE
Simone Dalton

The egrets existed as only folklore to me until I met Patricia. She is an aromachologist, someone who mixes essential oils to benefit one's beauty and behaviour. She lives in a small place called St. Lucia. On a recent visit to the island, my wife, Danielle, and I went to see Patricia about her oils. She gave us directions to the studio where she works as though we live there. A gap is a gap is a gap, I suppose. Caribbean people. We, and our countries, are different in the same ways.

Danielle drove as I tried and failed to make sense of a Google map that was not designed with gaps and small places in mind. *You see the blue beam coming from the dot? That's the direction we need to be heading in.* Danielle said this as a reader of maps. I turned the phone the other way as an asker of directions. We arrived, though it was still unclear where, but Danielle parked the car anyway. It was a dead-end residential street. A gap. There was no pavement, just patches of grass where the cars didn't pass. There was no drain either. Where does the water go when it rains? It doesn't.

The car was parked alongside the wall of a house with a woman peering out of a window. I knew she was not Patrica and decided that she belonged to the house and it to her because she did not look happy that we were there, in a car, on her grass. Or was it the government's grass? Ownership is at times uncertain in a small place. *Don't block tantie driveway, eh.* I touched Danielle's arm as I said this, urging her to inch the car up a little more.

Across the street there was a bright yellow-and-green house that looked like it was recently painted. The house shared the yard with another structure, one which stood in stark contrast to its mate. It was a two-storey building, more like a treehouse made of a patchwork of wooden sheets, stained a dark shade of brown both on purpose and due to the rain. Soon, we would discover that the treehouse belonged to Patricia, while she rented the other one as her home.

Patricia appeared in the doorway of the treehouse. As a certain kind of woman, I coveted her glowing, seemingly pore-free, caramel coloured skin. As another kind of woman, I was intoxicated. We were welcomed inside with hospitality reserved for prospective clients. Overjoyed at a newly minted deal with a hotel in America, she was effervescent as she applied 'West Indian Warmth' to my wrist, something else to my forearm, and yet another oil to my neck. Slick with scents, I was delighted until the mosquitoes arrived.

It was hard to leave Patricia, her personality, and her oils. As we idled in the yard between the yellow-and-green house and the wooden structure, I noticed the canopy of trees above our heads. *Cashew nut,* she offered, sensing my question before it was fully formed. *There're some over here too.* She was walking by the time she said this, pointing across the yard to a twisted jumble of vines, branches, and large dark-green leaves. *Here* led to a mangrove. On the other side of it ran the Castries-Gros Islet Highway. *Most mornings I try and come out early to watch the egrets.* Although life seemed to have left the river the mangrove grew in, the trees were thriving. But there were no egrets.

The November sun had begun its descent, but the egrets' call to return home was muted despite the waning hours of the day. There was still enough light for them to graze along the edges of the nearby marina. Once thought to be vagrants in the Caribbean, when sightings were a rare surprise, egrets are now a cosmopolitan species in the region, favouring swamplands for rest.

But they are not *of* the region, not in a biogeographic sense. Originally from Asia, Africa, and Europe, near extinction due to over-hunting and the plume trade (great egret, little egret), and a response to 'increased animal husbandry and intense agricultural practices' (cattle egret) are among the list of reasons for their migration.

✤

We share a migratory pull. My people, the ones I know of, have been leaving the Caribbean since the fifties. Their reasons are mixed. The stories of a few are rooted in trauma and poverty. Most, like my father, were caged birds that needed to be released to fly. All have incurred this debt as a price of progress.

Here is the thing about progress: it makes a pigeonhole of what matters. What is pushed to the periphery is left unattended. Suddenly, you wake up in a three-bedroom, two-and-half-bathroom bungalow in a suburb east or west of Toronto, unsure of whose bootstraps were cut for you to get there.

An Indigenous woman reminded me of this at an international women's conference in Vancouver last year. She shook as she told a colleague and me about a recent exchange she'd had with her university roommate from India. The latter woman had dreams of her foreign-student visa being turned into a permanent-resident card. Canada was her Promised Land. But she knew nothing about the land she had dreams of settling on. Nothing of the Wet'suwet'en Nation's land or the Attawapiskat, Nishnawbe Aski, and Eabametoong First Nations' land where the water is not safe to drink. *Don't you research a country before you move to it?* As her breath quickened, my own breath stopped. No. I did not research. In June 2008, Stephen Harper apologized to Canada's Indigenous Peoples for the brutal residential school system. I had taken the citizenship oath six months prior. Harper's apology and the injustices it was meant to acknowledge remained in my periphery. I had studied the booklet, gotten all the questions right, mumbled the oath – all for a place on the land. In the pursuit of progress, I had swallowed a regurgitated Canadian history as Truth. Malnourished, never did I question whose truth.

⚘

The egrets appeared later that evening, in the hundreds, and changed the landscape. Now dusted with white feathers, the mangrove hung even lower with the weight of the sleeping nesters. Cars with their sound systems blew past us, as we slowed down in our car to watch. For five minutes, maybe more, we sat with nothing more to do than pay attention.

I had not been paying attention, not in the way a writer ought to. Not, say, like writers Tanya Talaga, Ta-Nehisi Coates, and Sarah M. Brown do. Their interrogation of our humanity makes it possible for Greta Thunberg to flourish.

Austin Clarke, too, praised and practised paying attention. His version was a contact sport. He believed writers should let the world 'come at' them. I was told this one night in 2017 while sitting in a packed, windowless room on the University of Toronto campus. I was there for a conference commemorating Clarke's life, work, and legacy. The Barbadian-Canadian writer had died in 2016 after disrupting the canon. Dionne Brand, who sat a few chairs across from me, is known for her own way of answering this challenge. Her gaze upon the world can be described as one that registers angles – from the way she describes how people speak in the seaside village of Guayaguayare, where she was born, to how the Don Valley Parkway 'swallows sound.' It is a protracted process, paying attention in this way. That night, she appeared to receive Clarke's posthumous credo as a weight. A lingering sadness in her eyes said, *and there is still so much work to be done.*

Writers, artists of all expressions, do this work. Be it with words, brush strokes, the absence of light, or presence of musical notes, art has the power to make the invisible obvious. The power to reflect our beauty and our brokenness. To succeed takes attention, a gift Simone Weil called 'the rarest and purest form of generosity.'

Benevolence is admirable within the context of a world wrung by loss. And we have lost so many: people, places of rest, ways of being, histories. The count disorients. 'I have nothing soothing to tell you, that's not my job, my job is to revise and revise this bristling list, hourly,' Brand told us in *Inventory*. The job demands. While the losses have been great, the causes have been consistent: capitalism, colonialism, and environmental destruction. The perpetrator, simply human. In the face of what we have lost and continue to lose, attention becomes responsibility.

Ah, but let us not forget: I had not been paying attention, the writer *and* the human. We were both implicated, united by this flaw. The human did what humans sometimes do: exist rather than oppugn. This is the price of being preoccupied with the result and not the cause. This is what happens when you have been numbed into believing that circumstances – floods, droughts, pipe-borne diseases, escalating food prices – just happen and must keep happening because they have always happened and you have no power to stop them from happening. When you are trapped by a memory: The sky opened and targetless arrows of water rained down for spite. Everyone, everything, everywhere was in the line of fire. The foundation under your neighbour's house yawned. The trees and the soil around his house could not hold any more water because while the soil remained, the trees, the trees were gone. You watched the red dirt of the track your house sat on turn to red mud. One election season, a government official with a sense of humour named the track a trace, a word that indicates a road. The mud caked against the steps, up to the front door of your house. You waited. When a boldface flash of blue appeared in the sky, you dug. You did not have anywhere to put the mud, not since the last time, so you slung it to the next side until the sky was again pissed off.

The human blamed the rain, not who took the trees.

The human is from a small place; her memory is a mere harbinger of far worse memories of other humans from other small places. Places like Antigua and Barbuda.

The writer is a tourist. She soaks in the mud from sulphur springs for pleasure, hikes in rainstorms for spiritual release. She offers thoughts and prayers to a sky of an uninterrupted blue, hypnotized by the possibilities it whispers. She feels invincible, buoyed by her ability to 'get away,' to turn a memory into a muse. Without missing a beat, she turns on Spotify and sketches what she dreams. She plans for a house, on a hill, in a small place. Not a large house, just one that sits on land where she can grow trees for fruit and trees for beauty. Where she can hike to the summit, barefoot, with her notebook in one hand, while the other is perpetually sticky from the juice of mangoes.

It is only in the dreaming that it dawns on the writer: What will remain of the small place when she is ready to plant her first tree? Five, ten, fifteen years from now. A year, after the next hurricane. Will there be a hill? Or, will her bare feet succumb to the treeless, red mud, sinking until none of her remains to see the onset of darkness of the night or soft light of the next day. Unable to see the birds when they appear.

Did the writer learn nothing from the human?

Who said there will be birds?

I was struck by my unconsciousness as I stood before the egrets. *Unconscious: not knowing or perceiving; not aware; free from self-awareness* (Merriam-Webster online). What else had I not perceived that day, that week, that month, that year? Do the things not perceived necessitate their own inventory? A kind of list that reminds: 'The Earth is not our creation.' What could I tell Coates, the author of those words, about this place? What did I know of it, beyond what my privilege had allowed me to see?

My view of the egrets was compromised. Distance obscured them. I could not tell if they were great, little, or cattle egrets, or a combination of all three. I tried to squint, cursing my severe nearsightedness. Coupled with the insistence of passing traffic, my inquiry was futile. I knew they were asleep, with their dagger-like beaks concealed under feathery white plumes. But I could not see the length of their beaks or tell if the feathers were a courtship display.

The truth was that even if I had 20/20 vision I would still be clueless about the bird. The distance between the egrets and me may as well be as wide as the Caribbean Sea and the Atlantic Ocean. As Kyo Maclear wrote in *Birds Art Life*, 'What did I know of live birds? What did I know of the wild world, and what did it know of me?'

We had driven past the egrets each night, for at least a week, by that time. On our way to meals, errands, wrapped up in conversations about the arresting beauty of the island, never once seeing them. As I stood, outside the car, trying to capture a picture with my phone camera, two more egrets glided into position to complete the formation. Not a single leaf moved as they landed, not one that was perceptible to me.

The next day, and every day until we left St. Lucia, I sat on our balcony, looking out over Rodney Bay. There is a rhythm to the morning on the bay. It begins with a quiet that Jamaica Kincaid would call profound. There is a sense of safety in the noiselessness. The sky, the wind, the sea, all appear unchanged from one second to the next. It is as though they are impenetrable.

Now the birds, seagulls this time, appeared. Their beaks made staccato sounds, as they pierced the membrane of the water for fish. Sometimes the fish sacrificed themselves by jumping through the surface.

The water of the bay has many lives. It exists as the river we saw at Patricia's house, as the aqueous bed of the egrets in the mangrove, and as an invisible porter under the highway, carrying the discarded packages of unknown senders around the island.

The longer I sit on the balcony, the more likely I am to see the garbage that moves with the ebb and flow of the tide. It is easy to claim that the pollution does not exist, that it is an exaggeration. That there is no proof the plastic bags, bottles, or aluminium cans are responsible for the dwindling fish population. If one were to simply view the bay as a slideshow instead of a feature film, it would only appear pristine.

But the tide does change and it brings our dirty secrets with it.

The closing scene of the day from my balcony played like an allegory: a seemingly unmanned thatched boat-hut floated by the house, barely making a wake, only to be replaced moments later by a loud, gas-guzzling barge, delivering building supplies to the men working on houses around the bay.

The water connects all of us – people, animals, and things – in one way or another. This is also true of our choices. The ones we make about our own lives stretch beyond ourselves to become the inheritance of someone else.

🌿

I am the writer, the human, Patricia, and the egrets. I am the water, in the stillness of the bay and the churn of the hurricane. I am the waste that kills the fish. I am the seagull that kills the fish. I am the fish. I am the sun that scorches through the rain clouds. I am a small place.

Attention and consciousness are intimate yet different. Each functions for a unique purpose. Attention makes allowances for the deluge of data which confronts us daily by selecting the portion and not the whole. Unable to consume it all, things fall away, go unnoticed. The data that we will not attend to is neglected. We even question the existence of that which we cannot perceive.

Consciousness: the quality or state of being aware especially of something within oneself; the state or fact of being conscious of an external object, state, or fact; awareness, especially concern for some social or political cause (Merriam-Webster online). Consciousness, this is a high power. It is discernment, mirroring our lives against the current state of the world. It gives us the language to give voice to what we find. It asks: What do you care about? What will you stand up for?

Apocalyptic or benign – call the changes in our climate what you will, the semantics are irrelevant. The challenge of this time is a crisis of consciousness. We cannot care about what we do not believe; we cannot act if we are not aware.

In his 2012 Jefferson Lecture, the writer, environmental activist, and farmer Wendell E. Berry shared:

> For humans to have a responsible relationship to the world, they must imagine their places in it. To have a place, to live and belong in a place, to live from a place without destroying it, we must imagine it. By imagination we see it illuminated by its own unique character and by our love for it. By imagination we recognize with sympathy the fellow members, human and nonhuman, with whom we share our place.

By imagination, place is also redefined. This disruption removes the barriers that enable us to pay attention to the plight of some and not of others; it compels us to act for all and not for the one. 'I am' is an invitation to 'we are.' It is a call to collective consciousness. After all, a big place is just a collection of small places and 'we do not have to live as if we are alone.'

Wendell E. Berry, Jefferson Lecture, 2012, https://www.neh.gov/about/awards/jefferson-lecture/wendell-e-berry-biography

Dionne Brand, *Inventory*. (Toronto: McClelland & Stewart, 2006).

——, *Love Enough*. (Toronto: Vintage Canada, 2015).

Ta-Nehisi Coates, *Between the World and Me*. (New York: Spiegel & Grau, 2015).

Kyo Maclear, *Birds Art Life*. (Toronto: Anchor Canada, 2017).

Simone Weil, *Gravity and Grace*. (New York: Routledge Classics, 2002).

TRIPLE MOMENTS OF LIGHT & INDUSTRY
Brenda Hillman

During our protest at the refineries, our friend R tells us there are
bugs in the oil in the earth-colored vats at Valero & Shell, tiny bacteria
changing sulfides, ammonia, hydrocarbons, & phenol into levels of
toxin the mixture can tolerate, & then we consider how early tired
stars gave way to carbon molecules a short time after the start of time
& now carbon makes its way in all life as the present tense makes its
way in poetry, the sludge in the vats where the hydrocarbonoclastic
bacteria break things down to unending necessities
      of   which Dante writes

      of   the middle of hell

light   *where no light is*

R says his friend who tends the bugs for the company feels tenderly
toward his mini-sludge-eaters, they are his animals, he takes their
temperature & stirs them, & so on. We pause to think of it. Such
small creatures. At the beginning of life the cells were anaerobic,
ocean vents of fire, archaea, then they loved air. In the axis of time
there are triple moments when you look back, forward, or in. As a
child you were asked to perform more than you could manage. Your
need was not symmetrical. It is impossible to repay the labourers
who work so hard. R describes his friend's work as devotional. The
bacteria do not experience hurt or the void but their service is uneven
& that is why i protest.

THE PROSPECT
Marcella Durand

The prospect – to return to that word
and really think about it, dig into it, like how a word
can be like dirt, and can sprout something like green,
green all over, but still, the prospect, which implies
something incipient, and maybe something planned? Planning
for the future, something happening or about to happen along a line
of green woods, or green horizon, or just a green line

along the edge of what we can see, we who peer
out the window, and if you didn't know the window
was placed in the wall in a way to look out over
a line of green along the horizon almost like
it was coming toward you, that line, spreading toward us.

THE WAY CARRYING SOMEONE CHANGES HOW WE LOVE
Ruth Daniell

In the Pacific there is a mother orca who won't let go
of her dead baby. My first thought, though I don't want it,

is: how long would they have let me hold you?
I don't want to know the answer, though I have ideas,

scraps of information I must have read somewhere once
about newborns and palliative care and hospitals

and that I hope I'm never called upon to properly recall.
You're nine months old.

You've lived in the world barely longer
than you lived in my body. I love you so much.

It's that simple. While you are learning to
pull yourself to standing the news is full of Tahlequah

and her dead calf. For over two weeks she won't give up
her baby to the water. The research scientists worry

she'll exhaust herself by diving down to retrieve the body
when she loses control of it in rough waters.

I wonder how much she understands. Is it all grief
or does she have some wild hope that breath

can return to one who's gone? No. I don't wonder that.
Of course she knows in her heart what it means

that she cannot help her baby. Any parent would.
Dear one, I like to admire your wrists,

how pudgy you are that your wrists are merely rolls
where your arms and hands meet: slivers of pale skin

where the rest of you is tanned. The orca pod in Puget Sound
struggles to get enough to eat: the Chinook salmon are declining

and what fish there are to eat are contaminated by toxins
that are passed on to their offspring. I live in a world

in which giants like whales are delicate. You live here too.
I find it more difficult than I thought I would

to watch you grow, although of course I want you to,
to live and grow up and old. I'm melancholy every time

I fold your outgrown clothes and put them in storage.
You will never be my little baby again.

I try not to make everything about me. 'Grief
isn't owned by humans,' a biologist says,

watching Tahlequah carry her baby on her head
through the water. 'Does grief change once you've met

the being that you've carried?' she asks. Tahlequah's
calf was born alive: it swam by her side

and scientists are asking if grief is deeper
because of the time they had to swim together,

because there was a birthing experience,
because they bonded amongst the waves.

I don't know. Is that a question worth asking?
I remember my first pregnancy and its loss

almost obliterated me but of course I love you,
here and now, more than anyone else.

You're pulling my hair and wiggling your toes
as you nurse – your body, flung across my lap,

in a perfect little sundress, deep blue with bright pink
roses. I'll be so sad when you outgrow it.

Words are taken from quotes by Jenny Atkinson, executive director of the Whale Museum on San Juan Island, included in 'Grieving Mother Orca Carries Dead Calf for More Than a Week, Over Hundreds of Miles' by Samantha Raphelson on npr.org, July 2018.

THE OMEGA TRICK
Dani Couture

*I want this to be the last thing I'll ever do, to stop here
and say I'll go no further.*
— Kate Hall, 'Overnight a Horse Appeared'

A portside slap of white hieroglyph warns objects are larger
than they appear and do not disappear beneath the surface.
As if something that would dare that close would turn back.

This intent has legs. Too late, I've already forgotten
I can die. But if I did, it would be some signature trick:
a released fish knuckleballed into the lake and taken up
in flight. This desire to get close is all opposing mirrors –
the universe trying to both see and collapse into itself.

Some days, there exist two types of hunger,
except, in the end, only one. The first eats the other.

It's how I imagine these galaxies we're told to believe in
when I've never even been to California.

Upriver, a parade through a stalled parade of empty
buildings. Huge, clumsy machinations Oz'd with Model T
descendants. The waters no longer run red or court fire.
We've found better blends to run off. Crushed pills
in spoonfuls of corn syrup. Come, the algae blooms
are so thick, we can walk on water we can't drink.

At a certain hour, the sky and river look twinned,
an untilled grey, and I can understand how a plane can be
piloted into water thinking it was the right way up.

PERSPIRATION, A CONSPIRACY
Adam Dickinson

*37.8°C Internal temperature, 88 heartbeats per minute,
Oxygen Consumption (Litres per minute) 0.34*

*Cognitive test: This is a test of your ability to complete words
when some of the letters are missing; Detection Task Reaction
Time (ms) 238.6*

An early
draft
of a lubricant
for getting
the hell
out
the engineered
conclusion
in which
the flight
attendant
doctors
the drink
with an
emergency
exit
over the Canaries
trailing afterlives
like blisters
of a herpes
outbreak
or the punished
grin
of a lack
of means

swollen
marshmallows
are drooling
over the fire
their sunburns
follow
the predictable
misshapen plots
in the annals
of medical
science
trees
named
after ashes
were always
more likely
to get it
in the end
it's too sunny
to look directly
back
from where
we came
and now
our money
requires
huge fans
to keep it
cool

Note on the text:
How do we imagine writing with and about heat in a warming world?
What forms of writing might emerge when heat and its effects are

invited into the compositional process? With the assistance of the Environmental Ergonomics Laboratory at Brock University, I undertook several heat stress trials, raising my internal body temperature by around 1.5°C through active and passive heating. At various intervals, during all these trials, I wrote, took cognitive tests, and measured my core temperature, skin temperature, blood pressure, CO_2 uptake, and brain blood flow among other data. Using this data, I developed poems that approach the environment through the signifying framework of temperature extremes and respond to global warming as a future of addled, feverish thinking.

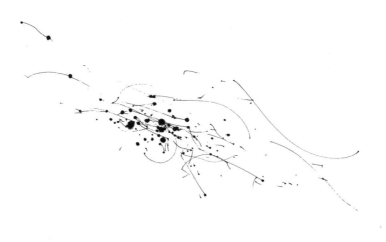

Sacha Archer, *Tree Sketch #1: Silver Maple, Acer sacchcirinum.* 45 min. 23.05.16.

Sacha Archer, *Tree Sketch #2: Cucumber Magnolia, Magnolia acuminate.* 180 min. 12.06.16.

KEBSQUASHESHING
Armand Garnet Ruffo

The Kebsquasheshing floats through my back door
carrying my youth, the fishing rod I dropped overboard
years ago, carrying the pike and their pike dreams
of barbless lures, fat worms, and clean water.

Today I tear into the *Globe and Mail* searching
for an article explaining why the transformer blew
spewing hundreds of gallons of PCBs
into the water. Discover no explanation.

Ontario Hydro blameless. No harm done.
And still we drink and the water continues
past us, past the newspaper, up and out to the Arctic.
Where big fish eat small fish and dream clean.

ENVIRONMENT
Armand Garnet Ruffo

I am asked to write something about the environment.
And so I ask myself, What does environment mean?
I google it   *The natural environment encompasses all*
                living and non-living things occurring naturally,
                meaning in this case not artificial. The term
                is most often applied to the Earth or some
                parts of Earth ...

The definition goes on and on, and I slip out of it and into
a long time ago when I got into a fight with my father
who in his absolute stupidity decided to dump the junk
from the back of his truck into the bush. Pointing to the shit
on the ground, he argued that everyone is doing it.

That afternoon he ended up slamming the tailgate shut
about to storm off while I picked up the stuff others
had forgotten, just as he had forgotten, failed to remember.
It was the first time I stood up to him. My legs trembling.

Definition from 'Natural environment,' Wikipedia.

LESSONS FROM PRISON: A SHACKLED PIPELINE PROTESTER REFLECTS
Rita Wong

My work for the past decade as a writer and scholar has been to learn with and from water – to follow what rivers and watersheds teach us. I love the Bow River, the Fraser River, the Peace River, the Columbia River, the Pacific Ocean, the Arctic Ocean, and all the watersheds that British Columbia and Alberta are part of.

How do I express this love?

On August 24, 2018, while BC was in a state of emergency because of record-breaking wildfires caused by climate change, I sang, prayed, and sat in ceremony for about half an hour in front of the Trans Mountain pipeline project's Westridge Marine Terminal. For this act of opposition to fossil-fuel expansion that no one can afford, on August 16, 2019, I was sentenced to twenty-eight days in prison by Judge Kenneth Affleck in the BC Supreme Court, as recommended by the Province of BC's Crown Prosecutor Monte Rattan.

After I left the courtroom, I was handcuffed, shackled, and transported in a chilly van with fellow political prisoner Will Offley. He, like me, had argued in our defence that our actions were motivated by necessity due to climate crisis. As I wrote in my sentencing statement, since the federal government has abdicated its responsibility to protect us despite full knowledge of this emergency, it became necessary to act. Our arguments were rejected by Judge Affleck.

Will was incarcerated at North Fraser Pretrial Centre while I was moved into an overly warm vehicle that ended up in the Alouette Correctional Centre for Women (ACCW) in Maple Ridge. The combination of heat and sliding around on the metal seat gave me motion sickness, so I'd vomited by the time I arrived at the prison.

I was born on Treaty 7 territory in what is also known as Calgary, and spent half my life there before moving to the unceded Coast Salish lands known as Vancouver. I love both places. I oppose pipeline expansion because I love the land known as Alberta, and see the urgent need to make a transition off fossil fuels.

I feel that the best way to repay my debt to the people who built the oil industry is not to automatically assume that oil is the only way Alberta can survive, but to lovingly assert that there are at least two things more important than oil: water, and life itself. As former Lieutenant Governor of Alberta, Grant MacEwan, pointed out in his last book, *Watershed: Reflections on Water*, 75 percent of the water in the Bow and Elbow Rivers comes from snow melt. When we accelerate that melting beyond a certain rate, we are guaranteed to melt the ice caps. Surely we are smarter and better than this.

This is why, since March 2018, I've spent a great deal of time up at Burnaby Mountain. I believe that everyone who lives on unceded Coast Salish lands has a responsibility to uphold Coast Salish laws, which entail respecting and protecting the land that gives us life.[1] This is why I was arrested and sentenced to time in prison.

My first night at ACCW was spent in maximum security. My cell (Charlie 9) had a bulletin board, on which a previous prisoner had left words: *COURAGE & SERENITY*. The lights never went off completely in my cell. I threw a sweatshirt over my eyes and slept from sheer exhaustion after writing a letter to friends and watching a bit of APTN on the television. It was a surprise and a pleasure to see Sharon McIvor on TV, talking about the regaining of status for Indigenous women who'd had it taken away by colonial legislative violence. In the morning, I was moved to medium security after breakfast. Though my stay in maximum security was short, I was treated kindly by my fellow inmates, one of whom gifted me a hair tie and another who showed me how the phone system worked.

In medium security, Birch A5, I had a cellmate, who showed me the ropes around the prison and even made us prison candy, a confection melted from creamer, sugar, and peanut-butter packets salvaged from the dining hall. Many of the women I met were struggling

---

1. https://twnsacredtrust.ca/about-us/

through various experiences of addiction, trauma, and poverty. Prison is not the best place to address these problems.

More programs are needed to support the healing and empowerment of inmates. Systemic discrimination results in the over-representation of Indigenous women and low-income women being incarcerated. One woman was a survivor of residential school abuse, another had been attacked on the Highway of Tears as a young teenager, another was four months pregnant and constantly hungry because the meal portions in prison were inadequate for someone who is eating for two. In the spirit of sharing whatever gifts I could, I facilitated a creative writing workshop, for the women there have powerful voices, stories that need to be shared.

I had the opportunity to work outside, tending the prison's grounds, pruning trees, and so forth. As I did, I kept thinking: Imagine what we could do if we diverted fossil-fuel subsidies – and billions wasted on destroying forests through disasters like the Site C dam – toward regenerating forests and the carbon sinks we need to cool this earth? What if we invested in local food security, regenerative agriculture, and diversifying genuinely renewable energy? Though our systems are currently failing us, I believe that the transformations we need are possible.

Prison was hard but bearable, and actually very educational in terms of how people navigate a systemically violent structure by helping each other get through these systems together with compassion and kindness in all kinds of small and big ways, notwithstanding personal and interpersonal dramas that come and go.

Many of the prisoners were hungry much of the time. Some women who didn't need as much food shared what they could with others who felt hungry, possibly because of the meds they were on to treat their addictions. The dining hall served food ranging from bologna sandwiches to chicken to hot dogs, and, for breakfast, toast, muffins, and porridge. Prisoners can supplement dining-hall meals with food purchased from the canteen. For a while, we could eat vegetables from the prison garden, though that privilege was arbitrarily withdrawn.

Note, however, prisoners who work are paid a starting wage of about two dollars a day, and you cannot buy very much for that. I was fortunate to have funds so that I could buy rice, cheese, popcorn, and junk food that I shared as much as I could, on the instructions of friends who put funds into my account. But if I'd relied only on the twenty dollars that I made for working ten days on horticulture in prison, I would not have been able to buy much. Indeed, I spent half of that twenty dollars on a ten-dollar yoga mat that I passed on to another prisoner when I left ACCW.

I had the privilege of being as well prepared as one might be for going to prison – I'd visited prisons as a volunteer for many years as part of Joint Effort[2] and Direct Action Against Refugee Exploitation. I also had information from previous prisoners who'd spent time at ACCW for their principled opposition to this pipeline expansion, women like long-time social-justice activist Jean Swanson, now a Vancouver city councillor. This helped me imagine what to expect and how to prepare for incarceration.

I wish I could be as well prepared for climate crisis. I'm not, though I'm trying my best to get prepared. For starters, I got arrested because we're in a climate emergency. We are in imminent peril if we consider the rate of change we are currently experiencing from a geological perspective. We are losing species at an alarming rate and many face mass extinction due to the climate crisis that humans have caused. This is the irreparable harm I sought to prevent, which the court, the Crown, and corporations also have a responsibility to prevent.

The courts' and the Crown's failure to prevent climate crisis is made clear by contrasting my four-week prison sentence with the few pitiful fines paid for the Trans Mountain Pipeline, which has had a much larger impact on the land than my small action by the Westridge Marine Terminal. Tickets I found online that were issued in Valemount and Fort St. John by the BC Oil and Gas Commission

---

2. http://prisonjustice.ca/joint-effort/

for $230 per violation – a slap on the wrist for the scale of work they're doing.

It feels like no one in any official capacity is effectively monitoring the criminal damage that the Trans Mountain pipeline has inflicted as its contractors cut down countless trees and destroy wildlife habitat. Meanwhile, concerned citizens who try to protect water and land are overpoliced. This disproportionate enforcement against individuals trying to prevent harm while turning a blind eye to corporations harming the land and water is systemic injustice.

Governments and systems that should be enforcing environmental-protections laws are failing us, and when I and other land and water protectors point this out, they penalize and scapegoat us instead of addressing how broken and ineffectual these systems are. It's surprising to find myself in the unexpected position of having spent time in a Canadian prison as a political prisoner, punished by the petro-state for asserting our responsibilities to care for the health of the land and water. The state is failing in its responsibility to protect the well-being of current and future generations, so it's up to everyday people to step up.

Spending time within the prison's walls taught me that there are good people caught in terrible systems, and that systems change is a necessary response to climate crisis. The women in prison are a microcosm of the larger challenges we have with addiction as a society. While poor women addicted to drugs are criminalized through policing that targets vulnerable individuals, other forms of addiction found in powerful, wealthy circles that are arguably as deadly or more deadly for humanity, have been given a free pass by the federal government.

I think addiction to oil – and the corporate structure that enables oil extraction that will lead to mass extinction – is something we as a society need to face and get over together.

We urgently need to return ourselves to health and balance, to what the land can teach us when we listen, to the lessons of the rivers, the ocean, the forests. We can be better relatives to one another.

Now is the time to stop poisoning the earth, and to create jobs that care for and renew the land instead of destroying it, as efforts like the Green New Deal work toward. Now is the time to leap.

Instead of rearranging chairs on the deck of the *Titanic*, we need to be building lifeboats. First Nations like the Tsleil-Waututh articulate the cultural shift needed to reduce our carbon footprint, helping us to make those lifeboats. As protectors of the Burrard Inlet, they do their sacred work for all our sakes. The very least we can do is reciprocate by contributing whatever gifts and skills we each bring toward the urgent goal of climate justice and the move to a renewable society.

I understand that the transition off oil is hard, yet it is technically possible, as the Solutions Project demonstrates.[3] Greta Thunberg and George Monbiot, too, have alerted us to the urgent need to support natural climate solutions at the scale required.[4]

Almost every day in prison, I would take the time to sit outside, watch the trees, and sing songs to thank the land. Gratitude, respect, and reciprocity with the land were what I decided to focus on while I was in prison. My body was restricted, but my heart, mind, and spirit were free. One time, we smudged briefly in the prison, standing in a circle and singing the women-warriors song, the bear song, and a song for the eagles. It was a quick ceremony before we had to get back to our unit for count and lockdown, but it reminded me of the healing walk for the tar sands[5] that I participated in years ago.

In the first year of that healing walk through the brutal devastation wrought by Suncor and Syncrude near Fort McMurray, immersed in gross, carcinogenic air, somehow we saw a bear and an eagle above us on the same day. The next year of the walk, the organizers made T-shirts with both the bear and the eagle on them, and I often wear this shirt to remind me what the healing walk has taught me.

---

3. https://thesolutionsproject.org

4. https://www.theguardian.com/environment/video/2019/sep/19/greta-thunberg-and-george-monbiot-make-short-film-on-solutions-to-the-climate-crisis-video

5. https://www.jstor.org/stable/41819673

The bear and the eagle represent courage and love, both of which guide us when we honour our reciprocal relationships with the land and water.

I was released from Alouette Correctional Centre for Women after eighteen days for good behaviour. I walked out with naloxone training, more mail than I've ever received in my life, and a renewed commitment to uphold natural and Indigenous laws. I went right back to Coast Salish Watch House at the perimeter of Trans Mountain's tank farm, where I continue to be active with the Mountain Protectors working group.[6]

People have asked me: *What can I do?* I say: *Don't give up.*

Find creative ways to stop the pipeline expansion, and turn it into a stranded asset.

Spend time with and protect sacred places like the Burrard Inlet,[7] the Peace Valley,[8] your local creeks and forests.

Our future depends on these acts of care and attention. Don't look away from the violence that Trans Mountain is inflicting.

At the same time, keep an eye on the solutions we need to build together, the lifeboats that are in the making.

A poem written in my cell:

prison candy

what poverty, confinement, & ingenuity produce –
a tasty brown taffy stretched
from packets of creamer, sugar, peanut butter
saved from dining-hall meals
mixed & microwaved
set & shared by inmates
after count in Birch
Camp Cupcake isn't as sweet as it sounds
lockdown is still lockdown
but sisterhood survives in it somehow
bright as a pink volleyball

bouncing off the sand
steady as a bear beyond the pines
chomping down on blackberries
in the prickly late-summer bramble
quick as a dragonfly
riding the unseen breeze
that brushes across our cheeks

6. https://www.facebook.com/mountainprotectors/
7. https://twnsacredtrust.ca/
8. http://peacevalley.ca/

FOR THOSE WHO CAN STILL AFFORD IT, GLACIERS WILL CONTINUE TO EXIST
Evie Shockley

yours is a cooler world

hermetic

sealed   the waters

do not rise toward your baseboards

and bassinets

nor do they brown   poisonous

or recede

a beach ~

its ocean   its sand ~

is a place you visit

at will   the towers of ice

remain high and mighty

in the distance

at your pleasure   you ski

or ignore them   your skies

produce rain that drops down

from some dark vault

beyond earth's closed-loop atmosphere

not renewable

but new   untouched even

by your imagination

xyqxyqxyqxythe rest of us bathe in your runoffqxyqxyqxyqxyqxyqxyqx
yqxyqxyqxyqdrink our own sweatxyqxyqxyqxyqxyqxyqxyqxyqxyqx
yqxyqxyqxyqdrown in the knowledgexyqxyqxyqxyqxyqxyqxyqxyqxyqx
yqxyqxyqxyqxyqxyqxyqxyqxyqxyqxyqxyqxyqxyqxyqxyqxyqxyqxyqxyq
xyqxyqxyqxyqxyqxythat without h$_2$oqxyqxyqxyqxyqxyqxyqxyqxyqx
yqxyqxyqxyqxyqxyqthere'll be hell$_2$payxyqxyqxyqxyqxyqxyqxyqxyq

> – *for agassiz, two ocean, logan, boulder, shepard,*
> *dixon, whitecrow, herbst, harris, and red eagle*

PORT BLOCKADE OVEN-HOT SWEET POTATO
Jane Shi

the moon was pregnant. blushing pink pearl embryo.
shifting bodies never meant to be anxious. blushes from
knowing sieves of our smiles. mouths are bowls, are
feasts, are watching it all happen. bowls can talk back,
hold the broken water, turn into a hand, a needle, a magic
spell to sew the river back together. i have seen

the soldiers before they come. they wear different uniforms.
they run with machine gun signs that read, 'we protest life,'
'we hate our own breath,' 'we hate our mother.' faces
trained not to twitch when we ask them to join us. cheekily,
i say, 'i hope your children abandon you.' and we will.

the moon is a huge flirt. i text her on Lex and tell her i'm
here. say, why can't i go to the water? she teases me.
tells me to wait until i'm ready. don't worry, you'll know.

the moon will bless us. the water is an archive of dreams.
is a tomorrow poem. is a together line break. is
the children
          of our children
                    of our children.

when i read poetry with Indigiqueer artists
when they offer me their kokum's rat root post PTSD attack
when they offer up their Advil for pain   or a place to escape
a shoulder to cry on
a friendship   the generosity of trust
and truth   despite me   taking
and taking
for over twenty years
the sky
above their homelands
the least i can do is join them when
the revolution is   only
a few blocks down

from this parasitic

and over-priced

basement suite   i call

home

JIA YOU
Jane Shi

putin marches chinese soldiers across shanghai streets.
fear the Uighur terrorists, jiuma warns me,
and no sooner, street stands steaming with nan and kebab
fold into the hollow sprawls of massage parlours, german furniture stores,
french bakeries, italian pubs, American sex toy shops,
local shoe shops doubling as sunday school, real
massage parlours, a lego construction of western carpets
and han ornaments. disappeared.

students tell each other before gaokao: 'jiayou.'
mothers tell their children before gaokao: 'jiayou.'
thick wallets tell their diasporic offspring before AP economics: 'jiayou.'

translation: build pipelines transporting oil between Skovorodino
and Daqing
translation: build pipelines transporting greed and colonialism across
Turtle Island

rupture water with oil.
drink oil-flavoured bbt with the thick straw of a gun barrel.
brush your teeth with bitumen paste, rinse
rinse
repeat.

extract it from skin browner than ours.
take it, drink it. until the sun never dares set
on our civilized, meddling kingdom.
yellow powder amalgamated with sheens of white –
xiaojie the fairest in the land. a quick nod,
scorching back scratcher: got you covered.
advancing grades, following orders, guaihaizi marching westward

until we lose ourselves between the failure of 89%
and the success of swearing allegiance to the queen
(making the last payment on the mortgage). filial, determined,
loyal to the very end.

there would be no chinese faces protesting pipelines that day.
I wonder if we'd need to drink poison from these waters we
steal from to see the filth on our hands. but
you cannot bribe a river to love you, forgive you,

no. not today.
because the Yangtze remembers the poppies that poisoned,
the villages evacuated, the children sold, the maozedongs and
elizabeths laundered exchanged transported.
just so little xingxing could go to school.
just so little favourite grandchild could have a better life.
just so we never have to talk about 49, 66–76, 89 tucked between
the eights in our addresses and phone numbers,
the ones and zeros of our pockets. just so.

you tell me,
'jia you.' but how can you
when you do not know the name of this river. when
you do not know where your bones will be buried.
when you have crushed your veins between big data and the sea.

just so we never have to talk about
what we pretend not to know.

a bottle of cooking oil, crushed by a tank.

_____

jia you means 'add oil,' another way to say 'good luck'
gaokao is the National Higher Education Entrance Examination, a prerequisite
exam to get into higher education in the People's Republic of China

WRITING IN A DANGEROUS TIME
Carrianne Leung

Of Beginnings

My social-media feeds have been filled with photos of bees. Bees on flowers. Bees in a ballet of flight. Bees on bees. My friends are obsessed with bees. In the context of the complexities and catastrophes facing us, of course we are obsessed with bees.

Simultaneous to the appearance of bees on Facebook, Instagram, Twitter, I keep trying to write, but it's not going well.

We writers know the power of the flow – that magical place where words pour from us like soft water. We intuitively feel for that surge that is from us but not quite of us. This is the part of the process of writing that makes our work so enlivening and occasionally terrifying. But when the words and stories do not flow, when we are caught in low tide, when floundering ... I have been floundering.

There is no magic to be found lately. Icebergs are melting, fire is setting the world alight, 50 percent of our biodiversity has been lost. The scale of human suffering is insurmountable. Hate crimes, incarcerated children, state terrorism, missing and murdered women, overpoliced bodies, people floating on water, people crying, people rising. We look for bees in our state of seeming helplessness with the sole duty to not look away. What do I write?

I don't know, and this essay will not give any answers, but I hope it gives us a space to think about, talk about, write toward something. Perhaps this essay is not even about writing. It may be more about being human, existing in this precipice of something else, some deep transformation, as our world is also transforming.

Of Looking

I started writing this paper in the spring. The days were growing warmer, the leaves on the trees burst into my favourite hues of fresh green, flowers re-emerged like Sleeping Beauties. Unlike my usual joy at greeting this season, I wondered what did I do to deserve this wonder?

One day, as I was walking, a monarch butterfly flew close, crossing my path. I stopped to give it the right of way, and it fluttered, in that zigzag way that butterflies do, past. I wanted to apologize for not having given full attention to their fierce tenacity often enough in my lifetime. I wished that I had paid better attention. Do butterflies know how beautiful they are to us? Do we know how beautiful we can be to each other?

We know that a writer needs to attend to the world, and I do. But I do so lately with an intensity that can only be described as a last gasp, as if all this will fall away like illusion at any moment, and I must remember to record it properly. I don't have the discerning eyes of a scientist who can perhaps detect the smallest evidence of our unravelling. I have the eyes of a writer who seeks only beauty, humanity, and life, even in scenes of death. Everything looks deeply sacred to me now – trees, birds, strangers' faces. There is an illumination to everything. Is this what mourning looks like? I am full of grief and fear and wonder.

What are we really looking for? Who are we becoming in this looking?

There are other things happening. My child turns twelve and starts middle school and is worried if they will have friends. My parents grow frail but attempt to be more kind. Some friends have just had babies, and I have to remember that babies are still being born. Who am I to despair? I am in the middle of life, a really good life that I may or may not deserve. I need to be called back to the minutiae of the everyday.

This is my predicament of being a writer in a dangerous time – the simultaneity of life and death on scales big and small … as I search for which stories to tell. What is to be said at this time? What is to be awakened, what essential truth is there to hold? I am only a storyteller, and all I've ever known has been that stories are necessary.

Of Language

Here I am in Nova Scotia, on an island off the bigger island where birds outnumber people. It's now August and I continue to struggle with my writing. Toni Morrison has died, and my social-media feed is full of her interviews, essays, and excerpts of her poetry and fiction. She leaves a stream of life in the wake of her passing.

The seagulls scream here, as I read Morrison's words on a rock by the shore. The sound interrupts my concentration, and I imagine that they are insistently repeating their history. I have been listening, but I can't understand their language, and I won't pretend that I ever will. I am here by the water and watch the many lifeforms, each with their own sense of place, time, and storytelling. The tide rises and falls regardless of whether I wake or die in the night. The rocks are unmoved by my presence. My brief visit is not even brief in their timeline but just a speck. I am a speck. This gives me some comfort.

Author and poet Dionne Brand claims that Morrison changed the texture of the English language, and I think this is what it takes in times like these.

Language is increasingly weaponized. We are and have always been engaged in a struggle over language and meaning. There have been warnings before – George Orwell's *1984* alerted us to how language can be co-opted from the people and delivered back as something else to contain the people. The Ministry of Love, Ministry of Truth, of Plenty were exemplary of what Orwell said was Oceania's doublethink. The Ministry of Truth, for example, was in charge of propaganda, the perpetual broadcasting and repetition of falsified histories, production of facts, the ultimate spin-doctoring.

We are in a storm of fascist language, I think. Hate gathers like fog and enunciates itself as policy, as rhetoric, as headline. Morrison asserts that this kind of language is not 'like' violence but very much is violence.

Part of what we do as writers is wrestle our language free of its institutional cages, its slogans and branding. We must create a sentence like Morrison or Brand to call attention to our humanity, wake us from this frozen state of hell, caress the texture of things. To sit with the noise of bees, of clover, of the scream of gulls, to listen even if we do not understand. I think of Morrison and her reach for language. I think of the sacred space as we, her readers, must reach to meet her. I understand language as my craft and my spell that I must invoke with careful intention. When we write, when we leave our marks on the page and our words walk off into other people's lives, I hope they bring a new way of being and seeing our humanity. I think of Morrison.

Of Violence

I can't turn away from the constant feed of evidence on my feed or the news. I have tried to log off social media. Not read the news. I do this because I do not know what to do in the face of so much violence. Everyday, there are fresh killings. Everyday, the news screams that we are in peril. I am so privileged that I can attempt to filter it out because my own safety is not as precarious as so many others', that of friends, those of people I love, that of strangers. The line from me to you, to them, to out there, to the bigger logic of things. These lines that connect all of us are becoming clearer. I am here only because 'they' are there in harm's way. There is a suffering that comes in bearing witness, in being unable to make it stop. We are not exempt, not safe, not innocent. There is no neutral place to exist or to write. But there never has been.

In an interview with author Thea Lim, Booker Prize–winner Marlon James stated that depictions of violence are gratuitous if we do not show its aftermath, the suffering and the survival. We seem to spectacularize violence. We know the brutality against Indigenous, Black, and brown people and communities. We know the trauma of widespread sexual and gendered violence in our institutions, our communities, our homes. We know so much and yet, violence is pornographic if we go numb. Thea Lim responds to Marlon James and extends that perhaps the flipside of violence is tenderness and intimacy. Perhaps then, this is the reach?

On Twitter, there was a post by Indigenous CBC journalist Jesse Wente that stayed with me. He wrote: 'Dystopian novels are not warnings, they are preparations.' And so, I rethink books like Nalo Hopkinson's *Brown Girl in the Ring*, Cherie Dimaline's *The Marrow Thieves*, Larissa Lai's *The Tiger Flu*. I also think of what Thea Lim told me about her novel *Ocean of Minutes* when I asked her if it was dystopia, and she replied that it was allegory.

In all these books, characters are forced to navigate a treacherous world, a world on the brink – but the central story is not about this. It's about what is required to survive. There is immense tenderness at the core of this survival, an expansive love that may not immediately topple the regimes but provide a path to sustain us on the way to doing so. These books offer an opportunity to re-imagine the world, draw on history and spirituality to refashion how to be human. And isn't that the whole point of literature? To show us to ourselves and keep pursuing this question: what does it mean to be human?

I think about Indigenous writers and Black writers whose works are not prophesying apocalypse because their communities are already post-apocalypse, or their apocalypse continues. Their lives through generations have already been devastatingly interrupted and they are bringing us life after. I think of BIPOC dystopian literature as perhaps not dystopian at all, and more as Afro- or Indigenous futurisms, especially the sci-fi literature. The power of imagination, the calling of ancestral knowledge to the fore, the inheritance of what it means to enact humanity – all this is in books. So, in times like these when I can't find words, I have always conversed with books. I am doing so again. I am learning. I am grateful.

Of Human

I tell my students, everything you write is about what it means to be human. Even if your characters are aliens, teenage vampires, cats, you are writing about humanity. Stories have always been my instruction manual on being human. When I first immigrated to Canada as a child, I learned English because I loved to read fiction. It wasn't a compulsion to communicate, but a compulsion to understand and a need to be reflected. One writer in particular, Jean Little, wrote of lonely children, children in pain, children growing up despite this loneliness and pain. I appreciated her so much because her stories were told against all the other narratives of childhood where I could not locate myself. I was in awe – how did this writer have this profound understanding of my feelings? How did she reach out from the page to remind me that I am part of a human family, not monstrous or Other, but just a child. I suppose this is the quest that I am on in writing this. I am seeking to know that I am not alone, and I am seeking to understand this pain and to put language like a salve upon it.

And it's not just a quest of suffering, but of putting the words to our complicated joy too. We mustn't forget about joy. We will need to reimagine what this means, reimagine what a good life is by other metrics.

Of Archive

I've been thinking about literature as archive. Literature is knowledge, document, testament to what a culture values and doesn't value at a given time. For that reason, some writers who do not see themselves in the pages write the absences, the blank space between lines, the margins. Every story that gets told is made possible by other stories that do not, could not come. These stories exist in silence, like ghosts, like haunting. I believe this is what makes someone like Toni Morrison a genius. Sonia Sanchez, in the documentary about Morrison titled *The Pieces I Am*, says that Morrison re-inserted Black ancestors into a 400-year-old archive of America in her novels despite the persistent erasure of Black life through slavery and anti-Blackness. She restored complex personhood and dignity to the lives of ancestors and descendants. Her work was archive.

In discussing Morrison's work, sociologist Avery Gordon writes in *Ghostly Matters* about ghosts and hauntings as power that can be named and not named, the density of concepts like capitalism, racism, colonialism, but also the delicacy of what these things feel like, sound like, act like in the lives of oppressed people.

We are thick with ghosts that can be named and not named. The recent surfacing of movements like #MeToo, Idle No More, and Black Lives Matter are giving shapes to ghosts, showing the outlines of absences, of the power that gives forms to our lives. It's not that gender violence, white-settler colonialism, or anti-Blackness are recent events but a trajectory of destruction that hides in policy, in rhetoric, in the everyday practices of ordinary people. It is not easy to write the delicacy of mundane violences, the artfulness of subjugation, the slow-death drive of hate and greed. These affects and effects are not so easy to describe, to name. So, we write the stories of these hauntings.

What gets read, what gets published, what gains traction are important questions to consider. If dominant stories that are repeated like some kind of truth are no longer working, if the assumptions about what is universal are proven untrue, we need counterstories, haunted stories, unburied stories. We need to clear space for them. Even in this moment when we face an uncertain future, or if we can't imagine what the human future will be, we must create and continue to serve this archive. The archive is for the past and the future, but also for now. It is hard to be human, it is hard to be a writer. Tell this.

Of Witness

We are changing necessarily. Our consciousness, our roles in history, our sensibilities – all are changing in these dangerous times.

If we are to write the world, to bring it in, let it permeate our words and blur the boundaries between text and life, what are the stories that must accompany us in this transition? To write, I must be filled with compassion. It's the only way I know how to do it. So, where does my compassion lie? I hope it will always be on the side of justice.

One of our functions as writers is to bear witness. Poet Billy-Ray Belcourt pushes us further and states that 'I think that part of the work of the poet in the twenty-first century in the West is to not just bear witness, but to trouble and de-normalize the way in which cruelty actually is a part of the fabric of life in Canada.'[1]

Does this goal seem lofty? Maybe. Is it necessary? Yes. Is it a dangerous time? It is. There is more at stake than ever, but perhaps this has always been so. Everywhere, throughout history, somebody has struggled for their lives and humanity, and somebody has picked up a pen, a paintbrush, used their voice to express this sorrow, this rage, this insistence to life.

Of Relationship

We need audacity in order to rewrite the world. But what kind of audacity? A hero's journey? I am rethinking this metaphor and narrative. I am turning the central protagonist around, so she can look at others, embrace them, engage, understand that she is born in a nest of relations and her heroism and courage is not a solo trek.

I hear Indigenous folks speak about a 'good way,' and I am trying to understand how to follow. Instead of being a 'good person' or a 'good writer,' I have started to think instead of fostering good relations. I count myself in the company of brilliant contemporary writers who are also wrestling with these preoccupations. The ideas weave like conversation in our stories, poetry, and essays. There is a genealogy in our literary histories, and this genealogy makes all things possible, generating language that I can hold and build. I believe our words are a commune also for readers. If we are dreaming

---

1. Adin Bresge, the Canadian Press, 'Hailed by CanLit, Poet Billy-Ray Belcourt Allies with Indigenous "Resistance,"' CTV News, Sept. 3, 2019, https://www.ctvnews.ca/entertainment/hailed-by-canlit-poet-billy-ray-belcourt-allies-with-indigenous-resistance-1.4575168.

the same dream – how miraculous, how incredible! Perhaps I have been hoping all along that I am working toward this same dream or a path toward something that feels like love, like life, like justice, like the human.

While I was writing *That Time I Loved You*, I felt a bit concerned by how my characters took over my life. They emerged as fully formed characters and followed me everywhere. I met Lee Maracle for the first time during the writing of the book, and asked her, in a scared whisper, if she ever felt she was haunted. Lee matter-of-factly replied, of course, writing is speaking to our ancestors. She accepts this as her practice. If this is indeed what we do – this divine invocation of ghosts, of history, our duty to ancestors – then perhaps we are also learning how to be good ancestors ourselves.

Writing possible futures must necessarily lead us back to the concept of relationship, and this includes non-human life forms. I have felt the need to slow things down, to walk at a snail's pace. On that encounter with the butterfly, I thought how strange that I offered a right of way to a butterfly, but isn't this so? Isn't this the most basic of things, the coterminous inhabitation of this space and time? Perhaps we can still retrieve and renew the possibilities of relationship that do no further harm, but can re-imagine the relationship between a woman and a butterfly that would exceed our understanding of the world as we know it?

I'll ask again: what audacity do we need now? I'll offer my answer: we need each other.

Of Story

Duty is not contrary to creative freedom. In fact, I think of it as part of creative freedom and the height of imagination. Story finds fertile ground when we understand what of ours is unique to tell. This does not mean borrowing or inhabiting another voice as the case of cultural appropriation. It is the acknowledgement of what is facing us vis-à-vis a web of relationships.

Some writers have written of dystopia, of the after-effects of catastrophe – whether this is a climate crash or a humanity crash. We also need to think about what to write in the time between, the transition, the ways we will change as we are changing. The change will be both rapid and slow. When I think of the time before Trump was elected, it could have been a million years ago. Or a minute. The temporal becomes something else in dangerous times when we are unprepared for how deeply we can sink, how deeply it cuts. And so, as writers, we play with time.

There is theory in storytelling, so there is deep knowledge found in our literature. Leanne Simpson writes that elders have said that everything we need to know is encoded in the structure, content, and context of Indigenous stories, including an ethics and responsibility.[2] And so, we need to make more space for these stories.

Even if you are not Indigenous or colonized, you may begin to free yourself from the confines of colonial logics, structures, forms, and return to the communal, to relationality. We, as Frantz Fanon indicated, must attend to the colonial wound. The wound that is also evident on the land, the waters that soon will no longer sustain us because of the same colonial and neoliberal violence that is and has been enacted on human bodies. We need to free our imagination from the trajectories of violence and destruction in order to write with an agency toward different futures.

If our work is not about this witnessing, touching on a deeper understanding of our humanity – a shared, dignified humanity for all of us – then what is it for? Dionne Brand says that we write in order to transform, and this touches me deeply. At the end, we need to banish the idea of a 'return' to safety … Perhaps the task is not to write ourselves back to an illusion but to a transformation. The role of writing, the role of art, has this special task.

---

2. Leanne Betasamosake Simpson, *Dancing On Our Turtle's Back: Stories of Nishnaabeg Re-Creation, Resurgence, and a New Emergence* (Winnipeg: ARP Books, 2011).

As we proceed, we will regather the most essential things, and we will write more love stories, comedies that are shot through our tragedies, our betrayals, our pride. I hope there will be new ways of seeing, thinking, loving, even as we remember. We will have choices to make: will we be generous? Will we be just? How will we act when we are afraid? Our literature will reflect all of this.

Of Endings, Of Futures

During one sleepless night while I waited for my child to be born, I learned that birth requires patience. I recalled that it was bloody, full of pain, full of euphoria, utterly magic. And so, now, I think maybe patience is required for all kinds of birth – to write, to listen, to die. Even in death, there is a process of creation, and so, even in this moment I remember there needs to be patience.

As I was finishing writing this, I read an article in the *Washington Post* by Dan Zak titled, '"Everything is not going to be OK": How to live with constant reminders that the earth is in trouble.' He writes, 'Hold the problem in your mind. Freak out, but don't put it down. Give it a quarter-turn. See it like a scientist, and as a poet. As a descendant. As an ancestor.'

I will be slow and patient, as I turn the problems in rotation and trust the stories are coming.

I have deep respect for the work of writers. We sit in solitude, in meditation and reflection for many hours of our days, crafting something exquisite that comes with pain, with joy, with tremendous purpose. Sometimes we turn to write as simply a way to relieve ourselves and our readers of this pain of existence, to offer shelter, and I do not mean to take away such necessary relief and shelter. But I do want to ask you, respectfully, gently, to not avert your gaze from the wounds of this world. I would like your participation in this project of what it means to be human in our fullest form, with each other, whether that be in your writing, in your relations, in your sense of yourself in the world.

I believe in the power of literature and the power of writers. We have a special opportunity and responsibility ahead. How privileged we are to be writers, how brave, how open we are to be the witness and the mirror! How lucky we are to be in a web of relations to everything! And also this: as much as the times we live in are dire, we are also fortunate to be the ones living in it.

It seems that we have some choices to make, it seems that we do this day by day, just as we will write it, word by word. I think we can be afraid, but I think we can also have courage.

I extend my hand to you. I watch this butterfly cross. I'll keep looking for bees.

ARTIST STATEMENTS

Sarah Mangle, *Weird* (p. 49)

When news of climate crises hit the mainstream in very real terms with the UN's IPCC in 2019, my anxiety hit the roof. I walked through my days expecting the world to collapse instantaneously. I couldn't stop reading the news. I was shocked there weren't immediate protests in the streets. I was confused by the interpersonal silence. I started making comics about the climate crisis to bring my anxieties to light, to give them space to breathe, and to start some conversations.

Jessica Houston, *Crossing the Line* (p. 50) and *The Greening* (p. 51)

The Horizon Felt photographs use colour to create new cartographies of the polar regions. Using the horizon and colours from the landscape as points of reference, Jessica Houston placed different coloured felt in front of her lens while photographing the north and south poles. Abandoned outposts, remote scientific stations, and retreating glaciers speak to the life of places and the storied matter that shapes them. These photographs take stock of the embedded histories of the poles and their entanglement of colonialism, capitalism, and environmental injustice, while opening up a space for rethinking the 'natural.'

Aude Moreau, *The Blue Line / La ligne bleue* (p. 52–53)

The Blue Line Project proposes to draw a line of blue light across the nighttime skyline of Lower Manhattan. Positioned at 65 metres[1] (213 feet) from the ground, the height of the glowing line will correspond to the projected sea level if all of the ice on the planet were to melt. Such a scenario is symbolic rather than realistic, since it does not relate to a scientifically predicted event as such, but acts instead to strongly promote environmental awareness.

This ambitious project solicits the co-operation of building owners and managers as well as residents, tenants, and their employees in a visually contiguous series of buildings in the Financial District. The project constitutes an invitation for a collaborative undertaking to realize a striking and poetic visual art work. At the same time, the simple fact of participating will engage those involved in a pertinent conversation about sustainability.

In this context, the choice of artistic intervention is one that operates from inside the urban architecture, creating a visual effect that engages the public space of the city outside.

---

1. J. L. Aspinall and J. L. Bamber. 'An expert judgement assessment of future sea level rise from the ice sheets.' *Nature Climate Change* 3, 424–427 (2013).

Shelley Niro, *Sleeping Warrior Dreams of Pastures and Power* **(p. 54) and** *Sleeping Warrior, Dressing Warrior* **(p. 55)**

Art to me is a body function. It begins with an urge and desire to manifest ideas. Sometimes the ideas come from a place that expresses innermost questions or observations. Mostly it develops out of a need to create and reflect my surroundings. The work is physical. It has to have a concentrated effort of muscle and material. Before I begin the whole process, the brain dips, dances, twirls, and jumps. It searches for areas left in the shadows. This is the most satisfying. There is a crossing of conjecture between body, brain, memory, and pigment. There are no distinct borders. Instead it warbles on the periphery of thought.

I am an Indian Artist from the Six Nations Reserve. I am Turtle Clan. I grew up in houses heated by wood stoves and no indoor plumbing. In some ways this felt limiting. However, looking back, it was a great training ground for the imagination. Hearing the wind blow through the cracks in the windows on winter nights, rain hitting the roof of the house, frogs and crickets in the summer singing all through twilight, and the night sky, its mass of stars with its infinite view, made for good opera, drama, and mystery. I was encouraged to listen, look, and learn from what was around and never take anything for granted.

Sarah Pereux, *The Canada Goose* **(p. 96) and 'Trinity' from** *Pretty Paws* **(p. 97)**

The Canada Goose is part of a series of graphite drawings that explore the theme of empathy, by manipulating symbolic animals associated with Canadian national identity. When I twist, break, and infest these animals, I explore my ability to empathize for these creatures; and I wonder if as a greater society, we have become desensitized to the suffering of the natural world.

Pretty Paws is a series of miniature graphite drawings, depicting severed beaver hands and feet with manicured nails. This series accentuates the natural lengthy shape of beaver claws by applying kitschy, over-the-top nail art. The application of this artificial beauty onto the decaying beaver appendages creates an uneasy tension by referring to the outstanding issue of cosmetic testing on animals.

Barry Pottle, *Under the Scope, Micro* **and** *Hopeful Antibodies* **(p. 153)**

We put climate change and global warming under the microscope – as an issue and as a priority. But I have to question how serious we are about it, as the microscope allows us to see things up close. Are we being serious about it or is it just for show, a pretty piece of ice with no real substance?

The COVID-19 pandemic has turned our world upside down and there's no doubt we are all in it together. This new world is far from what we know as normal and, as a society, it has challenged us in how we interact with each other. How we move in and out of our communities is at times confusing, discouraging, and negative. But I am hopeful we will find a cure and a way out of this pandemic. I am hopeful a vaccine and our cure will prevail!

Adam Gunn, *Ruin Value* (p. 154–155)
After Arnold Böcklin's third version of Isle of the Dead (1883). This was the starting point for my series of paintings on climate change. Böcklin's third version of a sinister, gloomy island cemetery isolated in calm waters is housed at the Alte Nationalgalerie in Berlin and was previously owned by Adolf Hitler, who hung it in the Reich Chancellery. I was contemplating the guilt Germans must have felt after the war and what their children must have thought about their parents' compliance or participation. I wondered if future generations will feel a similar way about us if we fail to do everything we can to avoid climate change. The title *Ruin Value* refers to the Albert Speer–pioneered concept of designing a building to leave aesthetically pleasing ruins when it eventually collapses.

Eshrat Erfanian, *Tres-pass 1* (p. 156) and *Tres-pass 3* (p. 157)
Tres-pass (2005–07), a series of fifteen digital photographs, depicts the landscape of Northern Ontario and Quebec. In recent history, this landscape was associated with mining industries in the late fifties and was particularly famous for its sources of uranium, but it is now in the process of being transformed into the site of a reclusive retirement paradise. Through pairing these images with addresses of oil refineries in the Middle East, Erfanian continues her exploration of the effect of text on image and the re-examination of the sublime migration of capital and manufacturing around the world.

Gaye Jackson, *Erratic #4* (p. 158) and *Erratic #8* (p. 159)
The photographic series *Erratics* consists of images of rocks that often appear out-of-place within their surroundings having been moved, sometimes great distances, by glaciers that once covered most of North America. I have been locating and photographing erratics in Northern Ontario since 2010. Because of their size and context, these boulders sometimes become physical markers that can guide the traveller, indicating place and direction in the landscape. The work reflects my interest in nature and landmarks, geology, and environmental history.

Kevin Adonis Browne, 'Decapitated Palms' (p. 178–179) and 'King Tide' (p. 180–181) from *The Coast*
The Coast: The aesthetics of environmental erasure – of what goes, what remains, and what is brought back to us on the tide.

Sacha Archer, *Tree Sketch #1: Silver Maple, Acer sacchcirinum* **and** *Tree Sketch #2: Cucumber Magnolia, Magnolia acuminate*

Tree Sketches were each composed by a different species of tree. As a writer connected to story, I felt it a salient action in this time of environmental crisis to step back and listen to the subjects I might otherwise have written over.

THE CONTRIBUTORS

Jordan Abel is a Nisga'a writer from Vancouver. He is the author of *The Place of Scraps* (winner of the Dorothy Livesay Poetry Prize), *Un/inhabited*, and *Injun* (winner of the Griffin Poetry Prize). Abel's latest project, NISHGA (forthcoming from McClelland & Stewart in 2021), is a deeply personal and autobiographical book that attempts to address the complications of contemporary Indigenous existence and the often invisible intergenerational impact of residential schools. Abel recently completed a PhD at Simon Fraser University, and is currently working as an Assistant Professor in the Department of English and Film Studies at the University of Alberta where he teaches Indigenous Literatures and Creative Writing.

Kazim Ali was born in the United Kingdom and was raised in Winnipeg and Jenpeg, Manitoba. His books include poetry, fiction, essay, memoir, criticism, and translation. After a career in public policy and organizing, Ali taught at various colleges and universities, including Oberlin College, Davidson College, St. Mary's College of California, and Naropa University. He is currently Professor of Literature at the University of California, San Diego. *Northern Light: Power, Land, and the Memory of Water* will be published in early 2021 by Goose Lane Editions in Canada and Milkweed in the US.

Hari Alluri (he/him/siya) is the author of *The Flayed City* (Kaya) and *Carving Ashes* (CiCAC/Thompson Rivers). A winner of the 2020 Leonard A. Slade, Jr. Poetry Fellowship for Poets of Color and an editor at Locked Horn Press, he has received grants from the BC Arts Council and the Canada Council for the Arts. His work appears in the *Poetry in Voice* anthology, and in *The Capilano Review*, *Poetry*, and PRISM *International*, among others.

Sacha Archer lives in Burlington, Ontario, with his wife and two daughters. Most recently, he has published *Mother's Milk* (Timglaset), *Lines of Sight* (nOIR:z), and MODELS *[of Economic Recovery]* (Simulacrum Press). Forthcoming publications include *Framing Poems* (Timglaset) and *UMO* (The Blasted Tree), a constraint based erasure/sound poem. Archer is the editor of Simulacrum Press (simulacrumpress.ca). His concrete poetry has been exhibited in the US, Italy, and Canada. Find him on Facebook and Instagram @sachaarcher.

Rae Armantrout is the author of fourteen books of poems, including *Wobble* (2018), a finalist for the National Book Award, *Partly, New and Selected Poems* (2016), and *Versed* (2009), which won the Pulitzer Prize and the National Book

Critics Circle Award in 2010. Her work appears in many journals and anthologies. She is professor emerita from UC San Diego and currently lives in the Seattle area. A new book, *Conjure*, will be published by Wesleyan in October.

Joanne Arnott is a Métis/mixed-blood author, editor, mother of many, Poetry Mentor for The Writers Studio (SFU), and Poetry Editor for EVENT *Magazine*. Joanne received the Gerald Lampert Award (1992), and the Vancouver Mayor's Award for Literary Arts (2017). Recent books include a poetry chapbook, *Pensive & beyond* (Nomados 2019), and a co-edited collection, *Honouring the Strength of Indian Women: Plays, Stories, Poetry* by Vera Manuel (with Coupall, Reder, and Manuel, University of Manitoba Press, 2019).

Oana Avasilichioaei interweaves poetry, translation, photography, sound, and performance to explore an expanded idea of language. Her six collections of poetry and poetry hybrids include *Limbinal* (Talonbooks, 2015) and *Eight Track* (Talonbooks, 2019); her recent sound-performance works are *Eight over Two* (2019, Semi Silent Award) and *Operator* (2018). She has translated nine books of poetry and prose from French and Romanian, including Catherine Lalonde's *The Faerie Devouring* (Book*hug 2018, QWF's Cole Foundation Prize for Translation).

Sâkihitowin Awâsis is a Michif Anishinaabe two-spirit water protector, geographer, and spoken-word artist from the Pine Marten Clan. She is a PhD candidate at Western University, where she studies Indigenous energy justice and pipeline resistance. She has contributed poetry to *Forever Loved: Exposing the Hidden Crisis of Missing and Murdered Indigenous Women and Girls in Canada* and is continually inspired by acts of decolonization, resurgence, and community healing.

Chris Bailey is a commercial fisherman from eastern Prince Edward Island. He has a MFA from the University of Guelph, and is a past recipient of the Milton Acorn Award for Poetry. His writing has appeared in *Brick, Grain, FreeFall,* and elsewhere, and has been translated into Italian. *What Your Hands Have Done*, his debut poetry collection, is available from Nightwood Editions.

Carleigh Baker is a nêhiyaw âpihtawikosisân/Icelandic writer who lives on the unceded territories of the xʷməθkʷəy̓əm, Skwxwu7mesh, and səl̓ilwəta peoples. Her debut story collection, *Bad Endings* (Anvil, 2017), won the City of Vancouver Book Award, and was also a finalist for the Rogers Writers' Trust Fiction Prize, the Emerging Indigenous Voices Award for fiction, and the BC Book Prizes Bill Duthie Booksellers' Choice Award. She teaches creative writing at Simon Fraser University.

Jonathan Ball holds a PhD in creative writing and is the author of eight books, including *Clockfire*, *The National Gallery*, and *The Lightning of Possible Storms*. He hosts the podcast *Writing the Wrong Way* and his first book, *Ex Machina* (a choose-your-own-adventure poem about how machines have changed what it means to be human) is available for free online at www.jonathanball.com/freebook.

Manahil Bandukwala is a Pakistani writer and artist currently based in Mississauga. She is co-lead of *Reth aur Reghistan*, a visual-literary exploration of Pakistani folklore that she is carrying out alongside her sister, Nimra. See more at sculpturalstorytelling.com. Her work has appeared in CV2, the *Malahat Review*, PRISM, and other places. In 2019, she won *Room* magazine's Emerging Writer Award, and was longlisted for the CBC Poetry Prize. She has two chapbooks, *Paper Doll* (Anstruther Press, 2019) and *Pipe Rose* (battleaxe press, 2018).

Gary Barwin is a writer and multimedia artist who lives in Hamilton, Ontario. He recently published *For It is a Pleasure and a Surprise to Breathe: New & Selected Poems* (Wolsak & Wynn) and *A Cemetery for Holes* (with Tom Prime; Gordon Hill). A new novel, *Nothing the Same, Everything Haunted: The Ballad of Motl the Cowboy* (Penguin Random House), will appear in 2021.

Yvonne Blomer is an award-winning poet and the author of the travel memoir *Sugar Ride: Cycling from Hanoi to Kuala Lumpur*. Her most recent book is *Sweet Water: Poems for the Watershed*, the second in a trilogy of poetry anthologies edited by Yvonne with a focus on water.

Nicole Brossard is a poet, novelist, and essayist born in Montréal. Among her books: *Mauve Desert, Notebook of Roses and Civilization, The Aerial Letter, Avant Desire: A Nicole Brossard Reader*. Co-director of the film *Some American Feminists*, she has won the Governor General's Award for her poetry twice and received the 2019 Lifetime Recognition Award from the Griffin Poetry Trust.

Kevin Adonis Browne is an award-winning Caribbean American photographer, writer, and speaker. He is the author of two books: *Tropic Tendencies: Rhetoric, Popular Culture, and the Anglophone Caribbean* (2013) and HIGH MAS: *Carnival and the Poetics of Caribbean Culture* (2018), which won the Bocas Prize in Caribbean Literature in 2019. He is also co-founder of the Caribbean Memory Project. He works at the University of the West Indies in St. Augustine, Trinidad.

Jenna Butler is an Albertan poet, essayist, editor, and professor. A woman of colour interested in multi-ethnic narratives of place, Butler teaches creative and environmental writing at Red Deer College and runs an off-grid organic farm.

Jody Chan is a writer, drummer, organizer, and therapist based in Toronto. They are the author of *haunt* (Damaged Goods Press), *all our futures* (PANK), and *sick*, winner of the 2018 St. Lawrence Book Award. They can be found online at www.jodychan.com and offline in bookstores or dog parks.

Ellen Chang-Richardson (she/her) is an award-winning poet, writer, editor, and community organizer of Taiwanese and Cambodian-Chinese descent. She is the author of two poetry chapbooks, *Unlucky Fours* (Anstruther Press) and *Assimilation Tactics* (Coven Editions), and her writing is forthcoming in *The Fiddlehead*, *third coast magazine*, *untethered magazine*, and more. The founder of Little Birds Poetry and the co-founder of Riverbed Reading Series, Ellen lives and works in Ottawa, Ontario on the traditional unceded territories of the Algonquin Anishinabeg First Nation. Follow her work at www.ehjchang.com.

Ching-In Chen is author of *The Heart's Traffic*, *recombinant*, *how to make black paper sing*, and *Kundiman for Kin :: Information Retrieval for Monsters*. Chen is co-editor of *The Revolution Starts at Home: Confronting Intimate Violence Within Activist Communities*. They have received fellowships from Kundiman, Lambda, Watering Hole, Can Serrat, and Imagining America, and are part of Macondo and Voices of Our Nations Arts Foundation writing communities. They teach at University of Washington Bothell. www.chinginchen.com

Margaret Christakos is attached to this earth. Her thirty-year creative practice includes a novel, a creative memoir (*Her Paraphernalia: On Motherlines, Sex/Blood/Loss, & Selfies*, Book*hug, 2016), and ten collections of poetry, including *charger* (Talonbooks, 2020), *Multitudes* (Coach House, 2013), and *What Stirs* (Coach House, 2008). Her work is included in *Regreen: New Canadian Ecological Poetry* (Your Scrivener Press, 2009).

Allison Cobb (pronouns she/her) is the author of *After We All Died* (Ahsahta Press), *Plastic: an autobiography* (Essay Press EP series, with a full-length edition forthcoming from Nightboat Books), *Born2* (Chax Press), and *Green-Wood* (originally published by Factory School with a new edition in 2018 from Nightboat Books). Cobb lives in Portland, Oregon, where she co-hosts *The Switch* reading, art, and performance series, and performs in the collaboration *Suspended Moment*.

CAConrad is the author of *Amanda Paradise* (Wave Books, 2021). Their book *While Standing in Line for Death* won a 2018 Lambda Literary Award. They also received a 2019 Creative Capital grant as well as a Pew Fellowship in the Arts Award, the Believer Magazine Book Award, and the Gil Ott Book Award. They regularly teach at Columbia University in New York City, and at Sandberg Art Institute in Amsterdam. Please view their books, essays, recordings, and the documentary *The Book of Conrad* (Delinquent Films) online at http://bit.ly/88CAConrad.

Dani Couture's most recent collection of poetry is *Listen Before Transmit* (Wolsak & Wynn, 2018).

Francine Cunningham is an award-winning Indigenous writer, artist, and educator. A graduate of the UBC Creative Writing MFA program, Cunningham's work was longlisted for the 2018 Edna Staebler Personal Essay Contest, won the 2019 Indigenous Voices Award for unpublished prose, and won the 2018 Short Grain Writing Contest. *On/Me* is her first book and has been shortlisted for the inaugural Jim Deva Prize for Writing that Provokes and the Indigenous Voices Award.

Jen Currin is the author of *Hider/Seeker: Stories*, which was named a *Globe and Mail* top 100 book of 2018. Jen has also published four poetry collections, including *The Inquisition Yours*, winner of the 2011 Audre Lorde Award for Lesbian Poetry, and *School*, a finalist for three awards. Jen lives on the unceded territories of the Qayqayt Nation (New Westminster), and teaches writing at Kwantlen Polytechnic University and the University of British Columbia.

Simone Dalton is a writer, arts educator, and recipient of the 2020 RBC Taylor Emerging Writer Prize. Her work is anthologized in *Black Writers Matter* and *The Unpublished City: Volume I*, a finalist for the 2018 Toronto Book Awards. As a memoirist, she explores themes of grief, inherited histories, race, class, and identity. In 2019, her play *VOWS* was produced for RARE Theatre's *Welcome to My Underworld*. She is currently working on her first book.

Ruth Daniell is a teacher, editor, and award-winning writer whose collection of poems, *The Brightest Thing* (Caitlin Press, 2019), explores fairy tales, violence, love, and healing. She lives with her family in Kelowna, BC, where she is at work on a second collection of poems about birds, climate change, parenthood, fear, and joy.

Adrian De Leon is a Los Angeles–based historian, poet, and essayist from Manila by way of Scarborough, Ontario. He is the author of two poetry collections: *Rouge* (2018) and *barangay* (forthcoming 2021). He is also the co-editor of *FEEL WAYS: A Scarborough Anthology* (2020). Adrian is an Assistant Professor of American Studies and Ethnicity at the University of Southern California, where he teaches courses on Asian American Studies.

Trynne Delaney (she/they) is currently holed up somewhere in Tio'tia:ke, growing plants and growing hair. You can read more of her work in GUTS *Magazine's* Movement Issue or listen to audio recordings of her poetry online. She recently received her MA from University of Calgary in English and Creative Writing. She hopes you're doing OK.

Adam Dickinson is the author of four books of poetry. His work has been nominated for awards including the Governor General's Award for Poetry, the Trillium Book Award for Poetry, and the Raymond Souster Award. He was also a finalist for the CBC Poetry Prize and the K. M. Hunter Artist Award in Literature. He teaches Creative Writing at Brock University in St. Catharines, Ontario.

Marcella Durand's most recent books include *The Prospect* (Delete Press, 2020) and her translation of Michèle Métail's book-length poem, *Earth's Horizons* (Black Square Editions, 2020). Other publications include *Rays of the Shadow* (Tent Editions, 2017); *Le Jardin de M. (The Garden of M.)*, with French translations by Olivier Brossard (joca seria, 2016); *Deep Eco Pré*, a collaboration with Tina Darragh (Little Red Leaves); AREA (Belladonna); and *Traffic & Weather* (Futurepoem), written during a residency at the Lower Manhattan Cultural Council. She is currently working on a new book-length poem, forthcoming from Black Square Editions.

Mercedes Eng is the author of *Mercenary English, Prison Industrial Complex Explodes*, winner of the Dorothy Livesay Poetry Prize, and *my yt mama*. Her writing has appeared in the Lambda-nominated anthology *Hustling Verse: An Anthology of Sex Workers' Poetry, Jacket 2, Asian American Literary Review, The Abolitionist, r/ally (No One Is Illegal)*, and *Surveillance* and *M'aidez* (Press Release).

Eshrat Erfanian is an artist and educator. She was born in Tehran and lives in Toronto. Erfanian's practice attempts to subvert the reading of the images generated by new technology. Her work ranges from video installation to digital photography and site-specific installations. Erfanian's work has been exhibited in the Jewish Museum in New York City, at Incheon Biennial, and in numerous galleries in Ottawa, Montreal, Vancouver, and Toronto. Her latest work is permanently installed at the Immigration Hallway in the Canadian Embassy in Paris. Erfanian is an alumnus of the ISP Whitney Museum of American Art and holds a PhD from York University in Toronto.

Whitney French is a storyteller and a multidisciplinary artist. She is the co-founder of Hush Harbour Press. She is also the editor of *Black Writers Matter* (University of Regina Press) and the creator of the nomadic workshop series

Writing While Black. The work featured is from her forthcoming science-fiction verse novel.

Elee Kraljii Gardiner and **Andrew McEwan** collaborate on the poetry project *Nature Building*, a reimagining of the Canadian canon. Her most recent book of poetry is *Trauma Head*. His is *If Pressed*.

Sue Goyette lives in K'jipuktuk (Halifax), the unceded, unsurrendered land of the Mi'kmaq peoples. She has published six books of poems and a novel. Her latest book, *Anthesis: a memoir*, is forthcoming from Gaspereau Press in 2020. She's been nominated for the 2014 Griffin Poetry Prize and the Governor General's Award, and has won several awards including the 2015 Lieutenant Governor of NS Masterworks Arts Award. Sue teaches in the Creative Writing Program at Dalhousie University.

Laurie D. Graham lives in Nogojiwanong/Peterborough, in the treaty territory of the Mississauga Anishinaabeg. Her books are *Rove* and *Settler Education*. An excerpt of 'Stone barn, fuel cloud ...' was published in 2018 in a chapbook collaboration with painter Amanda Rhodenizer called *The Larger Forgetting*.

Adam Gunn is a painter whose work focuses on interests in ideas about natural and unnatural orders with a deep concern for how an image is brought into being. Originally from Nova Scotia, he currently lives in Montreal. He has accumulated an MFA from Concordia University and a BFA from NSCAD University. He's been a semi-finalist in the RBC Canadian Painting Competition twice, and in 2019 completed a five-month residency in Berlin as part of the Nancy Petry Award.

Brenda Hillman is the author of ten books of poetry, including *Extra Hidden Life, among the Days* (2018), which won the Northern California Book Award. She has edited and co-translated over a dozen books, most recently *At Your Feet* by Brazilian poet Ana Cristina Cesar, which she co-translated with her mother Helen Hillman. Currently a Chancellor for the Academy of American Poets, Hillman is the Filippi Professor of Poetry at St. Mary's College of California.

Jessica Houston has travelled from pole to pole using objects, oral narratives, photography, and painting to evoke nature-culture entanglements. Her site-specific works collaboratively build knowledge, inviting viewers to listen to a variety of voices, including poets, penguins, and ecologists. She has received funding from the Canada Council for the Arts and her work is in the collections of the Montréal Museum of Fine Arts, BANQ, and the Museum of Fine Arts of Québec.

Gaye Jackson studied at the Northern Alberta Institute of Technology and the Ontario College of Art and Design, and has a BA (hons) in anthropology from the University of Guelph. Exhibited nationally and internationally, her work addresses issues around environmental history and land use, and has received critical attention through curatorial essays, reviews, and grants. Jackson, from Toronto, grew up in a small Ontario town in a family that encouraged exploration and a connection with the land.

Sheniz Janmohamed (MFA) is a poet, artist educator, and land artist who has performed in venues across the world, including the Jaipur Literature Festival, Alliance Française de Nairobi, and Aga Khan Museum. She is also the author of two collections of poetry: *Bleeding Light* (Mawenzi House, 2010) and *Firesmoke* (Mawenzi House, 2014). Her writing has been published in a number of journals, including *Quill & Quire, Arc Poetry Magazine*, and *Canadian Literature*.

Kaie Kellough is a poet, fiction writer, and sound performer. He has written for small and large musical ensembles and has performed internationally. His most recent book of poetry, *Magnetic Equator* (McClelland and Stewart, 2019), won the Griffin Poetry Prize. His latest work of fiction is the short-story collection *Dominoes at the Crossroads* (Véhicule Press, 2020).

Kirby's earlier chapbooks include *Cock & Soul, Bob's boy, The World is Fucked and Sometimes Beautiful, She's Having A Doris Day* (KFB, 2017), and *What Do You Want To Be Called?* (Anstruther, 2020). Their full-length debut, *This Is Where I Get Off*, is now in its second printing (Permanent Sleep, 2019) and currently being adapted for the stage. Kirby is the owner and publisher of knife | fork | book. www.jeffkirby.ca

Jónína Kirton is a Red River Métis/Icelandic poet and a graduate of Simon Fraser University's Writer's Studio. Her interest in the stories of her Métis and Icelandic ancestors is the common thread throughout much of her writing. She published her first book, *page as bone ~ ink as blood*, in 2015 at sixty years of age. Her second book, *An Honest Woman*, was a finalist in the Dorothy Livesay Poetry Prize. Both collections were published with Talonbooks.

Cory Lavender is a poet of Black Loyalist and European descent living in Nova Scotia, which is in Mi'kma'ki, the ancestral and unceded territory of the Mi'kmaq people. His work has appeared in journals such as *Riddle Fence, The New Quarterly*, and *The Dalhousie Review*. His chapbook *Lawson Roy's Revelation* came out with Gaspereau Press in 2018. His *Ballad of Bernie 'Bear' Roy* was recently published by knife | fork | book (2020).

Jessica Le is currently an undergrad student at Western University studying Business. Her work has been published in Western University's *Symposium Anthology*, RISE *Magazine*, and is forthcoming in the Cold Strawberries Collective's *Alternative Magazine*. She lives in Ottawa.

Curtis LeBlanc is a poet and fiction writer residing in Vancouver, BC. He is the author of *Little Wild* (Nightwood, 2018) and *Birding in the Glass Age of Isolation* (Nightwood, 2020). His work has appeared in *Joyland, Geist, Maclean's, The Malahat Review*, EVENT, PRISM *International, Prairie Fire, The Fiddlehead, Grain*, and elsewhere. He is the recipient of the Readers' Choice Award in the Poem of the Year competition by *Arc* and has been shortlisted for The Walrus Poetry Prize. He's also the co-founder and Managing Editor of Rahila's Ghost Press.

Christine Leclerc holds an MFA in Creative Writing from the University of British Columbia and has received a bpNichol Chapbook Award for the long poem *Oilywood*. She is a Physical Geography Major at Simon Fraser University. In 2019, Leclerc attended the UN Climate Change's COP25 to help promote climate literacy. She is interested in earth system response to climate forcing and climate justice. Currently, Leclerc co-investigates stream network dynamics as a NSERC-award recipient.

Karen Lee is most captivated by Voice. Sound. Beat. A lyrical storyteller, devoted to social justice. Lee is an accredited Jamaican Patois Court interpreter, voiceover artist, vocalist, and actor. Lee's poetry is published in *The Malahat Review, Humber Literary Review*, was commissioned for 'Toronto: Tributes + Tributaries, 1971–1989' at the AGO, and shortlisted for the Small Axe Literary Prize. *Tekkin' Back Tongue*, her poetry manuscript-in-progress, is inspired by her self-directed residency in Ghana and Kenya (2018). @karenleeartist on Facebook, Twitter, and Instagram.

Carrianne Leung is a fiction writer and educator. She holds a PhD in Sociology and Equity Studies from OISE/University of Toronto. Her debut novel, *The Wondrous Woo*, published by Inanna Publications, was shortlisted for the 2014 Toronto Book Awards. Her collection of linked stories, *That Time I Loved You*, was released in 2018 by HarperCollins and in 2019 in the US by Liveright Publishing. It received starred reviews from *Kirkus Reviews*, was named a best book of 2018 by CBC, and was awarded the Danuta Gleed Literary Award, shortlisted for the Toronto Book Awards, and longlisted for Canada Reads in 2019. Leung's work has also appeared in *The Puritan, Ricepaper, The Globe and Mail, Room* magazine, *Prairie Fire*, and on Open Book Ontario.

Natalie Lim is a Chinese-Canadian writer based in Vancouver, BC, and the winner of the 2018 CBC Poetry Prize. Her work is published or forthcoming in *Best Canadian Poetry 2020*, *Room* magazine, PRISM *International*, and more. She is an unashamed nerd and a believer in good bones, and you can find her on Twitter @nataliemlim.

Jessica Magonet is a poet and human rights lawyer who lives on unceded Coast Salish territories (Vancouver, BC). She is the author of *at this confluence* (Loft on Eighth, 2016). Jessica has been involved in the climate justice movement for many years with organizations including Ecojustice, the Sierra Youth Coalition, and the Climate Project.

Sarah Mangle's work is peopled with beautifully flawed characters. Her work is concerned with growth, feelings, shaky lines, and truth-telling. Her book-works, postcards, and zines are sold internationally. Her work has been featured in *The Globe and Mail*, *Hello Giggles*, *Shameless Magazine*, *Art/iculations*, *The Montreal Review of Books*, and *Broken Pencil*. During the COVID-19 pandemic, she offered free email art prompts to everyone, every single day.

Terese Mason Pierre is a writer and editor. Her work has appeared in *The Puritan*, *Quill & Quire*, and *Strange Horizons*, among others. She is currently the poetry editor of *Augur Magazine*, a Canadian speculative literature journal. Terese has also previously volunteered with Shab-e She'r poetry reading series, and facilitated creative writing workshops. She lives and works in Toronto.

Kathleen McCracken is the author of eight collections of poetry including *Blue Light, Bay and College*, shortlisted for the Governor General's Award for Poetry, and a bilingual English/Portuguese edition entitled *Double Self Portrait with Mirror: New and Selected Poems*. She was a finalist for the W. B. Yeats Society of New York Poetry Competition, the Montreal International Prize for Poetry, and The Walrus Poetry Prize. In 2019, she won the Seamus Heaney Award for New Writing.

Yohani Mendis is an emerging writer living in Toronto. Her work was shortlisted for the 2020 Edna Staebler Personal Essay Contest. Her work has appeared or is forthcoming in *The New Quarterly* and *The Hart House Review*. She is a student of the University of Toronto School of Continuing Studies Creative Writing program.

Aude Moreau holds a Masters in Visual Arts and Media from the Université du Québec à Montréal, and has developed a practice that encompasses her dual training in scenography and the visual arts. Moreau's work has been exhibited in

Canada and internationally. Her recent screenings and exhibitions have been held at the Rencontres internationnales Paris/Berlin (2020); Galerie antoine ertaskiran, Montreal (2018); Musée d'art contemporain de Montréal (2017); Casino Luxembourg – Forum d'art contemporain (2016); The Power Plant (2016); Canadian Cultural Centre, Paris (2015); and Galerie de l'UQAM, Montreal (2015). She has received awards including the Claudine and Stephen Bronfman Fellowship in Contemporary Art (2011), the Powerhouse Prize from La Centrale (2011), and the Prix Louis Comtois (2016). She lives and works in Montreal.

Tiffany Morris is a Mi'kmaw editor and writer of speculative poetry and fiction. She is the author of the chapbooks *Havoc in Silence* (Molten Molecular Minutiae, 2019) and *It Came From Seca Lake! Horror Poems from Sweet Valley High* (Ghost City Press, 2019). Her work has appeared in *Room Magazine, Prairie Fire, Augur Magazine*, and *Eye to the Telescope*, among others. She writes, edits, reads tarot, and hunts for UFOs in K'jipuktuk (Halifax), Nova Scotia.

Erín Moure is a poet and translator with eighteen books of poetry, a co-authored book of poetry, a volume of essays, a book of articles on translation, a biopoetics, and two memoirs, and is translator or co-translator of twenty-one poetry collections and two biopoetics from French, Galician, Portunhol, Portuguese, Spanish, and Ukrainian. A forty-year retrospective, *Planetary Noise: Selected Poetry of Erín Moure*, appeared in 2017 from Wesleyan University Press. Her latest book is *The Elements* (Anansi, 2019).

Shelley Niro is a member of the Six Nations Reserve, Bay of Quinte Mohawk, Turtle Clan. She is a multimedia artist, working in photography, painting, beadwork, and film. She is conscious of the impact post-colonial mediums have had on Indigenous people, and, like many artists from different Native communities, she works relentlessly to present people in realistic and explorative portrayals. Photo series such as *Mohawks in Beehives, This Land is Mime Land*, and *M: Stories of Women* are a few of this genre of artwork. Films include: *Honey Moccasin, It Starts with a Whisper, The Shirt, Kissed by Lightning*, and *Robert's Paintings*. Recently, she finished her film *The Incredible 25th Year of Mitzi Bearclaw*. Shelley graduated from the Ontario College of Art with Honours, and received her MFA from the University of Western Ontario. She was the inaugural recipient of the Aboriginal Arts Award presented through the Ontario Arts Council in 2012. In 2017, Niro received the Governor General's Award, the Scotiabank Photography Award, and the Hnatyshyn Foundation REVEAL Award. Niro recently received an honorary doctorate from the OCAD University and was named the 2019 Laureate of the Paul de Hueck and Norman Walford Career Achievement Award for photography.

Kunjana Parashar is a poet living in Mumbai. Her poems appear or are forthcoming in *Poetry Northwest, Borderlands: Texas Poetry Review, MORIA, Bengaluru Review, 45th Parallel,* and elsewhere. You can find her on Twitter @wolfwasp.

Sarah Pereux is an artist and curator working in Toronto. She recently received her Bachelor of Arts and a Certificate in Curatorial Studies from the joint Art and Art History program at the University of Toronto Mississauga and Sheridan College. She is a founder and co-curator of the Tiny Fist Gallery, located within Sheridan College, Trafalgar Campus. Working primarily in drawing and sculpture, Pereux explores issues of environmental ethics while critiquing consumerist trends and kitsch.

Barry Pottle is an Inuk artist originally Nunatsiavut, NL, now living in Ottawa, ON. Pottle has always been interested in photography as a medium of artistic expression and as a way of exploring the world around him. Through the camera's lens, Pottle showcases the uniqueness of the urban Inuit community. Whether it is at a cultural gathering, family outings, or in the solitude of nature that photography allows, he captures the essence of Inuit life outside Inuit Nunangat.

Jana Prikryl is the author of *No Matter* (Tim Duggan Books, 2019) and *The After Party* (Tim Duggan Books, 2016). Her work has received support from the Guggenheim Foundation, the Radcliffe Institute for Advanced Study, and the Canada Council for the Arts. Born in the former Czechoslovakia, she was a child when her family immigrated to Canada. She works as a senior editor and poetry editor at *The New York Review of Books.*

Nikki Reimer is a carbon-based life form / fifth-generation settler of Ukrainian and Russian Mennonite descent who resides on the traditional territories of the people of the Treaty 7 region in Southern Alberta. Reimer writes poetry, nonfiction, and micro-reviews, and dabbles in multidisciplinary art practices. Published books are *My Heart is a Rose Manhattan* (Talonbooks, 2019), *DOWNVERSE* (Talonbooks, 2014), and *[sic]* (Frontenac House, 2010). Visit reimerwrites.com.

Ira Reinhart-Smith is a sixteen-year-old activist living in rural Nova Scotia, or its true name, Mi'kma'ki. In 2018, Ira began to get more involved with the Fridays For Future movement. With the help of two others, he organized dozens of school strikes and spoke with multiple politicians to help deal with the climate crisis. In October 2019, Ira joined a youth lawsuit against the Federal Government of Canada for its failure to act on climate change. He and fourteen other inspiring youths are alleging that the Canadian government is violating their charter rights to life, liberty, and security of the person.

Waubgeshig Rice is an author and journalist from Wasauksing First Nation, an Anishinaabe community on Georgian Bay. His most recent novel, *Moon of the Crusted Snow*, is a national bestseller. He graduated from Ryerson University's journalism program in 2002, and spent the bulk of his news and current-affairs career at CBC in Winnipeg, Toronto, Ottawa, and Sudbury. He currently lives in Sudbury with his wife and two sons.

Erin Robinsong is a poet and interdisciplinary artist working with ecological imagination. Her debut collection of poetry, *Rag Cosmology*, won the 2017 A. M. Klein Prize for Poetry, and her chapbooks include *Liquidity* (House House Press, 2020). Collaborative performance works with Andréa de Keijzer and Hanna Sybille Müller include *This ritual is not an accident* (2016), *Facing away from that which is coming* (2017), and *Polymorphic Microbe Bodies* (2020). Originally from Cortes Island, Erin lives in Montréal.

Armand Garnet Ruffo was born in the Oji-Cree territory of Northern Ontario and is a member of the Chapleau Cree Fox Lake First Nation. His publications include *Norval Morrisseau: Man Changing into Thunderbird* (2014) and *Treaty#* (2019), both finalists for Governor General's Literary Awards. His latest project is collaborative film, 'On the Day the World Begins Again,' a video-poem about the incarceration of Indigenous peoples. He teaches at Queen's University in Kingston.

Krishnakumar Sankaran is a writer in Mississauga, Canada. His work has been published in *Strange Horizons*, *Cha: An Asian Literary Journal*, *Kindle Magazine*, and *nether*. In India, he was shortlisted for the Srinivas Rayaprol Poetry Prize, 2011.

Emily Schultz will publish her newest novel, *Little Threats*, in fall 2020 with G. P. Putnam's Sons. Her novel, *The Blondes*, was released in Canada with Doubleday, in the US with Picador, in France with Editions Alto and Editions Asphalte. Named a best book of 2015 by NPR and Kirkus, it recently became a scripted podcast starring Madeline Zima. Her poems have appeared in *Minola Review*, *rust + moth*, *Humber Literary Review*, and *Taddle Creek*.

Jane Shi is a queer Chinese settler living on the unceded, traditional, and ancestral territories of the Musqueam, Squamish, and Tsleil-Waututh First Nations. Her writing has appeared in *Briarpatch Magazine*, *Canthius*, *The Malahat Review*, *PRISM*, and *Room*, among others. She wants to live in a world where love is not a limited resource, land is not mined, hearts are not filched, and bodies are not violated. Find her online @pipagaopoetry.

Evie Shockley is the author, most recently, of *semiautomatic*, which was finalist for the Pulitzer and L.A. Times Book Prizes and winner of the Hurston/Wright Legacy Award. Among her honours are the Lannan Poetry Award and a fellowship from the Radcliffe Institute for Advanced Study. She launches joy, knowledge, and dissent into the world from her home base in Jersey City, NJ, and is Professor of English at Rutgers University.

Sue Sinclair lives alongside the Wolostoq River in Fredericton, New Brunswick, where she teaches creative writing and is editor of *The Fiddlehead*. She is the author of five books of poetry, most recently *Heaven's Thieves*, winner of the 2016 Pat Lowther Award.

Adam Sol's most recent book is *How a Poem Moves: A Field Guide for Readers of Poetry* (ECW Press, 2019). He is also the author of four books of poetry, with one on the way from ECW Press in 2021. He teaches at the University of Toronto's Victoria College, where he is the Coordinator of the Creative Expression and Society program.

Pablo Strauss has translated nine works of Quebec fiction into English including, most recently, *Of Vengeance*, *The Dishwasher*, and *The Country Will Bring Us No Peace*. His shorter translations, reviews, and essays have appeared in *Granta*, *Geist*, and *The Montreal Review of Books*. Pablo grew up in Victoria, BC, and has lived in Quebec City for fifteen years.

Anna Swanson is a writer and public librarian living in St. John's, NL. Her first book of poetry, *The Nights Also*, won the Gerald Lampert Award and a Lambda Literary Award.

Christiane Vadnais was born in 1986 in Quebec City. Before publishing her critically acclaimed first novel, *Faunes*, she worked for years in the literary community as an events programmer and project manager. *Faunes*, a collection of linked stories, is set in a post-climate-change future where humans struggle with a mysterious epidemic while other species adapt and proliferate. The English translation, *Fauna*, is published by Coach House Books.

At nineteen, **Isabella Wang** is the author of *On Forgetting a Language* (Baseline Press, 2019) and *Pebble Swing* (Nightwood Editions, forthcoming 2021). Her poetry and prose have appeared in over thirty literary journals including *Prairie Fire*, *The Fiddlehead*, and *Arc Poetry Magazine*, as well as four anthologies. She is the editor for issue 44.2 of *Room* magazine.

Rita Wong is the author of five books of poetry and an associate professor in the Faculty of Culture and Community at Emily Carr University of Art and Design on the unceded Coast Salish territories also known as Vancouver. She co-edited the anthology *Downstream: Reimagining Water* with Dorothy Christian.

Jacob Wren makes literature, performances, and exhibitions. His books include: *Polyamorous Love Song, Rich and Poor,* and *Authenticity is a Feeling.* As co-artistic director of the Montreal-based interdisciplinary group PME-ART he has co-created performances such as: *En français comme en anglais, it's easy to criticize, Individualism was a Mistake, The DJ Who Gave Too Much Information,* and *Every Song I've Ever Written.* His internet presence is often defined by a fondness for quotations.

THE EDITORS

Madhur Anand is the author of the collection of poems *A New Index for Predicting Catastrophes* (McClelland & Stewart) and the 'memoir-in-halves' *This Red Line Goes Straight to Your Heart* (Strange Light). She co-edited *Regreen: New Canadian Ecological Poetry* (Scrivener Press) and co-authored the scientific text *Climate Change Biology* (CABI). She is a full professor of ecology and sustainability at the University of Guelph.

Stephen Collis is the author of a dozen books of poetry and prose, including *The Commons* (Talonbooks, 2008), the BC Book Prize–winning *On the Material* (Talonbooks, 2010), *Once in Blockadia* (Talonbooks, 2016), and *Almost Islands: Phyllis Webb and the Pursuit of the Unwritten* (Talonbooks, 2018). In 2019, he was awarded the Latner Writers' Trust of Canada Poetry Prize in recognition of his body of work. In 2021, Talonbooks will publish *A History of the Theories of Rain*. He lives near Vancouver, on unceded Coast Salish territory, and teaches poetry and poetics at Simon Fraser University.

Jennifer Dorner is currently the Executive Producer of POP Montreal International Music Festival and has led arts organizations as director, curator, and artist since completing her MFA at Western University in 2001. From 2014 to 2019, she was the director of the Faculty of Fine Arts Gallery at Concordia University. Jennifer was appointed to the Board of the Canada Council for the Arts for a four-year term, effective June 2017 to June 2021.

Catherine Graham is the author of the award-winning novel *Quarry* and six acclaimed poetry collections including *The Celery Forest*, a CBC Best Book of the Year. She teaches creative writing at the University of Toronto where she won an Excellence in Teaching Award. Published internationally, she is a previous winner of TIFA's Poetry NOW and leads their monthly book club. *Æther: an out-of-body lyric* and her second novel, *The Most Cunning Heart*, are forthcoming. www.catherinegraham.com @catgrahampoet

Elena Johnson is the author of *Field Notes for the Alpine Tundra* (Gaspereau, 2015), a collection of poems written at a remote ecology research station in the Yukon. She has been a finalist for the CBC Literary Awards and the Alfred G. Bailey Prize, and holds degrees in Environmental Studies and Creative Writing. In addition to working as a writer and editor, she is a lifelong advocate for social, environmental, and disability justice. She lives on unceded Coast Salish territory.

Canisia Lubrin is a writer, editor, critic, and teacher. Her two books are *Voodoo Hypothesis* (Wolsak & Wynn, 2017) and *The Dyzgraphxst* (McClelland & Stewart, 2020). Her debut collection of short fiction is forthcoming.

Kim Mannix is a poet, fiction writer, and journalist from Saskatoon, Saskatchewan, who now resides on Treaty 6 territory in Sherwood Park, Alberta. Her work has appeared in numerous journals, anthologies magazines and newspapers across Canada and the US. She has two children who motivate and inform her work, and is deeply grateful to and concerned for the earth that mothers us all.

Kathryn Mockler Kathryn Mockler is the author of five books of poetry and several short films and videos. Her most recent publication is a poetry chapbook *Me Then You Then Me Then* (knife | fork | book, 2020) written in collaboration with Gary Barwin. Her debut collection of stories is forthcoming from Book*hug in 2022. She is the publisher of the Watch Your Head website.

June Pak was born in Seoul, South Korea, and now lives in Toronto, Canada. Coming from her personal experience of living in Canada as a Korean-Canadian, the hyphenated identity is a central theme in her practice. Her multidisciplinary works have been shown in Canada and abroad. She was awarded the K. M. Hunter Artist Award in Visual Arts (2004) and the Chalmers Arts Fellowship for her research in non-ethnic Koreans in Korea (2017).

Sina Queyras is the author most recently of *My Ariel*.

Shazia Hafiz Ramji is the author of *Port of Being*, a finalist for the 2019 Vancouver Book Award, BC Book Prizes (Dorothy Livesay Poetry Prize), Gerald Lampert Memorial Award, and winner of the Robert Kroetsch Award for Innovative Poetry. She was named a 'writer to watch' by the CBC, and her poetry and prose have been nominated for the 2020 Pushcart Prizes. She is at work on a novel.

Rasiqra Revulva is a queer femme writer, multimedia artist, editor, musician, performer, SciComm advocate, and one half of the experimental electronic duo *The Databats* (Slice Records, Melbourne; Toronto). She has published two chapbooks of glitch-illustrated poetry: *Cephalopography* (words(on)pages press, 2016) and *If You Forget the Whipped Cream, You're No Good As A Woman* (Gap Riot Press, 2018). *Cephalopography 2.0* (Wolsak & Wynn, 2020) is her debut collection. Learn more at @rasiqra_revulva, @thedatabats, and www.rasiqrarevulva.com.

Yusuf Saadi's first collection is *Pluviophile* (Nightwood Editions, 2020), which was selected for the CBC's summer reading list. He previously won *The Malahat*

Review's 2016 Far Horizons Award for Poetry and the 2016 Vallum Chapbook Award. At other times, his writing has appeared in literary journals including *Vallum, Brick, Best Canadian Poetry 2019, Best Canadian Poetry 2018, Canadian Notes & Queries, Arc, CV2, Grain, The Puritan,* and PRISM *International.* Yusuf holds an MA from the University of Victoria and currently resides in Montreal.

Sanchari Sur is a PhD candidate in English at Wilfrid Laurier University. Their writing can be found in *Joyland, Al Jazeera,* the Toronto Book Award–shortlisted *The Unpublished City* (Book*hug, 2017), PRISM *International,* EVENT, *Room, Flare, This Magazine,* and elsewhere. They are a recipient of a 2018 Lambda Literary Fellowship in fiction, a 2019 Banff residency (with *Electric Literature*), and *Arc Poetry Magazine*'s 2020 Critics' Desk Award for a Feature Review.

Jacqueline Valencia is a Toronto-based writer, essayist, and activist who earned her Honours BA in English at the University of Toronto. Jacqueline is the organizer of the 2015 Toronto Poetry Talks: Racism and Sexism in the Craft. She is a project partner at Poetry inPrint and former senior literary editor at *The Rusty Toque, Watch Your Head,* and *manygenderedmothers.* She is currently on the editorial board (acting acquisitions editor for 2020) of Insomniac Press, and is the founding editor of Critical Focus.

Thanks to Alana Wilcox, Crystal Sikma, Ingrid Paulson, James Lindsay, Tali Voron, and everyone at Coach House Books who helped make this ambitious and important project possible.

CREDITS

p. 36. 'Humpbacks, Howe Sound' by Kathleen McCracken, originally published in *The Constancy of Objects* (Penumbra Press, 1988), and appeared in *Double Self Portrait with Mirror: New and Selected Poems (1978–2014)* (Editora Ex Machina, 2014).

p. 38. 'High School Fever' by Kaie Kellough, from *Magnetic Equator*, copyright © 2019 Kaie Kellough. Reprinted by permission of McClelland & Stewart, a division of Penguin Random House Canada Limited. All rights reserved.

p. 44. 'Together we will rise or fall' by Jónína Kirton, originally published as 'For the Birds' in *Migration Songs* (Nose in Book, 2015).

p. 46. 'On Growth' copyright © 2020 by Rae Armantrout, originally published in *Poem-a-Day* on May 8, 2020, by the Academy of American Poets, Poets.org.

p. 48. 'Speculative Fiction' by Rae Armantrout, originally published in *Lana Turner No. 8*.

p. 52. *The Blue Line / La Ligne Bleue* by Aude Moreau first appeared in *La Nuit Politique / The Political Nightfall* (Montreal: Galerie de l'UQAM, 2015).

p. 56. 'Reclaiming Our Names' by Waubgeshig Rice, originally published online on waub.ca.

p. 62. 'For the Feral Splendour that Remains' by CAConrad, originally published in *Poetry* in January 2020.

p. 66. 'halfling bear (eclipse)' by Joanne Arnott, originally published in *Halfling Spring: An Internet Romance* (Kegedonce Press, 2013).

p. 69. 'soft body tidalectics' by Whitney French, first appeared in *Canthius*, Issue 02, Spring/Summer, as 'XIX – story of death by O' (2016).

p. 72. 'I never got over sixty likes' by Kirby, originally published in *What Do You Want to be Called* (Anstruther Press, 2020).

p. 78. 'The Larger Forgetting' by Laurie D. Graham is an excerpt from *The Larger Forgetting* (2018).

p. 80. 'Rhapsodic Trip' by Jen Currin, originally published in *filling Station*, issue 66 (2017).

p. 82. 'Grey Water' by Carleigh Baker, first published in *Bad Endings* (Anvil Press, 2017).

p. 93. 'The World Ends for Good This Time' by Manahil Bandukwala, originally published in the *Poets Resist* series on December 12, 2019 (*Glass: A Journal of Poetry*).

p. 98. 'Flotsam' by Sheniz Janmohamed, first published in *Firesmoke* (Mawenzi House, 2014).

p. 99. 'Lantern Letter: a Zuihitsu' by Ching-In Chen, first published in *Split this Rock* on August 26, 2019.

p. 101. 'The Poplar Vote' by Kazim Ali. Excerpt was originally published in *Northern Light: Power, Land, and the Memory of Water*, copyright © 2021 by Kazim Ali. Reprinted by permission of Goose Lane Editions and Milkweed Editions.

p. 116. 'How to Small' by Oana Avasilichioaei and Erín Moure, originally published in *Expeditions of a Chimæra* (Book*hug, 2009).

p. 121. 'Anemone' by Erin Robinsong, published in *Liquidity* (House House Press, 2020), originally published in *Effects Journal #2*, Fall 2019.

p. 123. 'On Radiance' by Adrian De Leon, originally published in *Dear Scarborough*, edited by Hiba Abdallah (Doris McCarthy Gallery, 2019).

p. 128. 'Amateur Kitten Dreaming Solar Energy' by Jacob Wren is an excerpt from a novel-in-progress by the same name.

p. 130. 'how to survive in a time of great urgency' by Jody Chan, originally published in *NightBlock* in 2019.

p. 136. 'Ashen Fields' by Ira Reinhart-Smith, first published in *Our Future, Our Story*, ofos.ca.

p. 137. 'Requies' by Christiane Vadnais and translated by Pablo Strauss, originally published in *Fauna* (Coach House Books, 2020).

p. 152. '26' by Kunjana Parashar, originally published in *SWIMM Every Day* on February 20, 2020.

p. 156. 'Tres-pass' by Eshrat Erfanian, first published in *Prefix Photo Magazine*, Autumn/Winter (Prefix Institute of Contemporary Art, 2012).

p. 158. 'Erratics' by Gaye Jackson, first published in *Prefix Photo Magazine*, Autumn/Winter Issue (Prefix Institute of Contemporary Art, 2014).

p. 160. 'Planet at the Crossroads' by Christine Leclerc wa originally published by Ricochet Media (https://ricochet.media) on December 5, 2019, and is reprinted with permission. 'Revolution' by Jessica Magonet first appeared in *Long Lunch / Quick Reads Anthology* and *at this confluence* (Loft on Eighth, 2016).

p. 165. 'How to Find Your Way in Strathcona County' by Curtis Leblanc, originally published in *Little Wild* (Nightwood Editions, 2018).

p. 166. 'refrain' by Hari Alluri, originally published in *Carving Ashes* (CiCAC, 2013).

p. 178. 'Tide King' by Kevin Adonis Browne, originally published in *Caribbean Quarterly*, 63:4 (2017).

p. 182. 'This Poem is a Dead Zone' by Krishnakumar Sankaran, originally published in *Strange Horizons* on August 3, 2020.

p. 187. 'Safety Net' by Yohani Mendis, originally published in *The Hart House Review,* Winter Supplement, on February 4, 2020.

p. 191. 'Spawning Grounds' by Isabella Wang, first published in *Geez Magazine*, Issue 52. 'Sandcastle Bucket,' 'Listen,' and 'Shoreline' by Isabella Wang, first published in *Contemporary Verse 2*, Issue 41.4 in Spring 2019.

p. 195. 'Meltwater Basin' by Ellen Chang-Richardson, originally published in *Ricepaper Magazine* on July 4, 2019.

p. 201. 'Snapshot (pg. 35)' and 'Snapshot (pg. 89)' from *NO MATTER: POEMS* by Jana Prikryl, copyright © 2019 by Jana Prikryl. Used by permission of Tim Duggan Books, an imprint of Random House, a division of Penguin Random House LLC. All rights reserved.

p. 203. 'Forty-nine,' 'Fifty-five,' and 'Fifty-six' by Sue Goyette are excerpts from *Ocean* (Gaspereau, 2013).

p. 217. 'Triple Moments of Light & Industry' from *Extra Hidden Life, Among the Days* © 2018 by Brenda Hillman. Published by Wesleyan University Press. Reprinted with permission.

p. 219. 'The Prospect' by Marcella Durand is an excerpt from *The Prospect* (Delete Press, 2020).

p. 222. 'The Omega Trick' by Dani Couture, originally published in *Listen Before Transmit* (Wolsak & Wynn, 2018).

p. 223. 'Tree Sketch #1' and 'Tree Sketch #2' by Sacha Archer, published by *The Blasted Tree* in 2017.

p. 227. 'Kebsquasheshing' by Armand Garnet Ruffo, originally published in *Opening in the Sky* (Theytus Books, 1994).

p. 229. 'Lessons from Prison: A Shackled Pipeline Protester Reflects' by Rita Wong, first published in *The Tyee* on September 24, 2019.

Typeset in Arno and DIN

Printed at the old Coach House on bpNichol Lane in Toronto, Ontario, on
Rolland Opaque Natural paper, which was manufactured, acid-free, in Saint-
Jérôme, Quebec, from 30 percent recycled paper, and it was printed with
vegetable-based ink on a 1972 Heidelberg KORD offset litho press. Its pages were
folded on a Baumfolder, gathered by hand, bound on a Sulby Auto-Minabinda,
and trimmed on a Polar single-knife cutter.

Cover design by Ingrid Paulson
Interior design by Crystal Sikma

Coach House Books
80 bpNichol Lane
Toronto ON M5S 3J4
Canada

416 979 2217
800 367 6360

mail@chbooks.com
www.chbooks.com